The Visual Marketer

By Jim MacLeod

Dedicated to my dad.

Thank you.

ISBN: 979-8-9911630-8-8 (Paperback)

ISBN: 979-8-9911630-9-5 (Hardcover)

ISBN: 979-8-9917616-0-4 (EPUB)

TILT
PUBLISHING

Tilt Publishing
700 Park Offices Drive, Suite 250
Research Triangle, NC 27709

THE
VISUAL
MARKETER

The Marketer's Crash Course for Creating Memorable and Effective Visuals

JIM MACLEOD

Table of Contents

Foreword

By Mark Schaefer, author of
"Audacious: How Humans Will Win in an AI Marketing World"

I can read your mind.

Really. Give me a chance.

If you're a marketing / advertising professional reading this book, you go to work with one thing pounding in your brain every day: "See me. See my work. Find us." The Marketer's Prayer.

Did I get it right? This is more than a Universal Pain Point—it's our collective crisis. We're all drowning in an AI-driven pandemic of dull, a content swamp that's getting deeper and darker by the nanosecond. Every executive alive faces the greatest challenge in marketing history: earning attention and awareness in a fractured and overwhelming cosmos of content.

I've studied this for more than a decade. In 2014, I warned about "Content Shock"—a world where deep pockets would win the war for attention. And I was right... until November 30, 2022, when ChatGPT crashed the party, ushering in the era of generative AI. Now, for less than a Grand Slam breakfast at Denny's, an algorithmic servant creates any content, any visual element you can imagine.

What's a word stronger than "Content Shock?" Content Catastrophe?

With AI nipping at the heels of every creator, we need a path forward. That's why I'm delighted Jim MacLeod picked up the torch to light a path of hope for us.

Jim starts from a smart position: Competent doesn't cut it. Competent is a commodity. The obvious is obsolete.

Even as AI democratizes artistry, the human who masters the science and psychology of visual content will make a quantum leap over the Canva hackers and template traffickers.

This is the perfect book for our chaotic age. Practical ideas steeped in data and insight, seasoned with the spice of artistic inspiration.

Jim brings to life a critical truth: in a world where sameness is abundant, standing out is an act of audacity. And standing out visually is no longer a choice; it's essential. Marketers today are not only storytellers but experience designers. We are called to create moments that stop the scroll, spark curiosity, and make a genuine connection.

Visual marketing strategy transcends tactics. It demands purpose, consistency, and raw authenticity. Jim takes us beyond the surface, deep into brand coherence and human perception. He gives us permission—no, he demands—that we break free from marketing's ivory tower, take bold risks, and claim the white space where creativity transforms brands.

Jim's book isn't just a "how-to." It frames a revolution. It's telling us that in the age of infinite content, the scarcest resource isn't creativity—it's wisdom.

And that's worth more than a million MidJourney masterpieces or Canva templates.

—Mark Schaefer

Introduction

It's almost 10:00 a.m. on Friday. You've gone through the necessary morning emails and you're settling into your day. You have a full day of work on your docket before you can start your weekend. The familiar chime of your email rings, and you see a subject line that begins with the word "URGENT." All caps = not good.

A coworker tells you that your boss just told him about a rush ad campaign that has to go out today. It's tied to an executive event. Registrations are below expectations, and you've been tapped to create the campaign. Due to the timeframe, you also have to create the graphics. The executive team will see this, so it has to be great. Even though you lack the time, budget, or skills to produce this, you're still on the hook to deliver the campaign.

As marketers, we've had to "do more with less" for years. We're always expected to do more while spending less time and money to achieve those enhanced results. One area feeling the squeeze right now is the final output of marketing content.

How often have you been expected to produce collateral quickly and with a limited budget, like in the scenario above? I'm willing to wager it's more than you'd like (sorry for starting off with a trauma trigger).

Have you noticed the design part sometimes falls on you? You're expected to create visuals that make an impact, but you've been given no formal training. Platforms like Canva, Stencil, and generative AI will say anyone can be a designer, but there's much more to it than just pasting copy and inserting an image into a template.

Tools are one thing. Experience is another. You've been given a task and only half of what you need to complete it.

Sure, you can use these DIY tools to pump something out, but it's probably not moving the needle the way you or your bosses want. These automated or templatized visuals are generic because everyone with a subscription can access them.

You still need to know how to craft marketing content that stands out, engages with your audience, and aligns with your brand. It's so much more than just "use visuals."

I attended a big marketing conference a few years ago and chatted with another attendee. She had just come from a session I wanted to attend, but I had a conflict. The session was based on a topic I was very interested in. When I asked my new friend how the session was, she was blunt.

"It was a 45-minute presentation that just told us we should use images in our social posts." She paused before sarcastically adding, "No $hit."

She was annoyed that she had wasted her time being told something that was common knowledge. You've spent time in marketing (or simply looked at the world around you), so you already know that using visuals is a great way to grab attention.

But now, you're expected to produce content with rich visuals. Plus, you have to create content that performs well. Granted, content with visuals is 94% more likely to be seen than text-based content.[1] It's one thing to be seen; it's another to get the viewer to take the action you want.

Everyone is trying to find a way to stand out in a noisy world. Many businesses prefer to play it safe and fit in with the rest of their industry. There's a reason why this is called playing it safe. You can't play it too safe if you're trying to stand out. It makes me think of the old adage, "Nobody ever got fired for buying IBM." True, but nobody got promoted, either.

You need to stand out if you want to get noticed.

Look at the energy drink industry. Many of the top brands are promoting an image that their caffeine/sugar potion is edgy, in-your-face, and extreme. Yet, the clear industry leader, Red Bull, uses an entirely different tactic with its visual marketing.

Figure 1: Three different energy drink ads

They're all selling the same essential product. However, each business took different approaches to reach the audience. Red Bull participates in the extreme sports arena with an F1 team and has previously teamed with the X Games. It still works to attract that core audience. The difference is the "Red Bull Gives You Wings" campaign is lighter and goes after a different audience.

Are you an industry leader who is playing defense? Or do you work for a challenger brand trying to gain market share? Either way, you must find ways to expand beyond your core audience. Visual marketing can be the fastest way to capture the attention of a new segment that your competitors have overlooked.

Fitting in doesn't help you stand out. Nowhere is this statement more true than when it pertains to visuals.

This book will help you learn how to stand out while keeping within your brand guidelines. Brand guidelines help you define a space that you can own. From a marketing or brand standpoint, what is uniquely yours that your competitors can't touch? Colors? Typography? Imagery? Animations? There are many ways to mark your territory visually.

Once you've established your territory with your target audience, what else can you do with visuals that will help your marketing efforts? A lot. You're already unique. Now, show that uniqueness to people.

So, why should you trust me?

About a decade ago, Neal Schafer, a renowned marketing author, consultant, and speaker, contacted me. He was organizing a new conference and wanted me to speak at it. He invited me because he said I had a story he hadn't heard before: a designer who later became a marketer. At the time, I didn't think my career arc was that unique. Over the years, I've talked to many marketers who admitted their jobs would be easier if they had my design background.

I originally studied design and found myself working with some great marketers across the startup, enterprise, and agency spaces. Being in rooms with these people helped me realize that marketing fascinated me. It was a whole new way to challenge the creative and analytical sides of my brain.

I was in these rooms because I learned how visuals can amplify marketing and tell a more memorable story. I have been fortunate to work for some leaders who understand the real value of design. Not every boss appreciates design, but those who do are more successful. According to McKinsey and Company, companies with top-quartile design outperform industry-benchmark growth by as much as two to one and returns to shareholders are almost double those companies who don't rank well for using design.[2]

Design, a large part of visual marketing, is more critical than many leaders know. But since you picked up this book, you must have a good idea.

So, why exactly did you pick up this book?

I hope it's because you understand that visuals can improve your marketing and want to get a leg up on your competition.

My goal is to go beyond the obvious. I'm not going to talk about Apple's marketing. They're great and you can find that in every other marketing book. I'll explain why nothing engages an audience like visuals. You'll also learn why much of your existing marketing know-how can be applied to visual marketing. If you've worked on personas, funnels, or user journeys, you can map that information to visual marketing.

As I mentioned, there are tools out there that can help you create visual content. Canva, Adobe Express, Stencil, and others promote themselves as design tools for non-designers. Anyone can indeed create middle-of-the-road content. But I know you want to create great content.

I'll introduce you to these tools and a few others. More importantly, you'll learn the basics that people without a formal design education often miss.

I wrote this book for marketers, but if you're a designer looking to expand into marketing, you'll start to see how your skills have prepared you for this switch. You're already a lot closer than you realize.

Visual marketing is more than just making something pretty. It's about crafting a compelling story that speaks to your target audience and compels them to take action.

Do you know why people react positively to certain types of photos?

How about the differences in color meanings across different cultures?

What steps of the creative process are you missing?

How often should you audit your content?

What tools should you use to create visuals?

Why is consistency more important than creativity when building a brand?

These are just a few questions you'll be able to answer by the time you're done. Answering these questions and dozens of others will make your marketing more effective.

This book will introduce you to the basic principles of design and provide actionable steps to improve your visual marketing. Some sections may cover concepts you're already familiar with, but I've connected marketing basics to the best ways to use visuals in your activities and deliverables. Feel free to jump around and focus on the areas most relevant to you today, then return to other sections as new needs arise.

If you're pressed for time and just want to learn about the different content types you can use, check out Chapter 11. Want to see what tools are available to DIY marketers? Jump to Chapter 10 to get an overview of tools for non-designers. Each chapter has a summary of key points you can use to see if you want to dig deeper into that topic.

Ready?

I know I am!

CHAPTER 1:

The Essence of Visual Marketing

"Make it simple. Make it memorable. Make it inviting to look at."

—*Leo Burnett*

Consistency is the most essential part of visual marketing. If there's one thing you need to learn: being consistent is more important than being creative. There's no doubt that creativity is essential to successful visual marketing. The only way creativity does its job is through consistent use.

Find something that works, and then keep doing that.

It sounds simple, right? Unfortunately, it's not. Creative people always want to try new things and take chances. However, marketing is about presenting a consistent message to prospects and customers to build reputation and trust.

And consistency works! Research from Techipedia shows that brands with consistent messaging are worth 20% more than those always trying new things.[1]

Be creative, but also be consistent. It may seem boring, yet your prospects and customers are not exposed to your marketing as often as you are. Nobody is asking why Nike hasn't updated its logo in decades. It works, so Nike keeps doing it (see what I did there?).

Definition and importance of visual marketing in the digital era

Visuals didn't matter as much when marketing was limited to print publications and radio. Obviously, radio doesn't include visuals, so we can skip past that part. Newspapers initially prevented the use of brand colors because they were limited to black, white, and gray tones. It wasn't until 1930 that color in magazines became common. Our great-grandparents would be overwhelmed by the amount of color we have in our lives.

As technology evolved, we saw the introduction of movies and television, both of which started in black and white and added color as time passed. Today, in the digital era, there aren't any limits when it comes to color. In fact, marketing in two dimensions is no longer a limitation.

Visual marketing is more important than ever since we have so much competition for our attention. If you think about the hundreds of marketing messages we are exposed to each day, you can start to grasp how difficult it is to cut through the noise.[2]

Visual marketing is about connecting your marketing messages with images, videos, and other visual assets to strengthen your brand. Visual marketing stands at the intersection of content marketing and brand marketing.

The broad scope of visual marketing within the overall content marketing strategy

Visual marketing needs to be at the heart of most of your marketing, especially in the areas of content marketing and brand marketing. The right visuals can tie all of your content together. It lets the viewer know that everything they see that looks like your visual marketing is connected.

THE ESSENCE OF VISUAL MARKETING

Assuming you're putting out high-quality content, as time goes on, a consistent visual identity with your content creates brand affinity. People learn that when they see your visual marketing, they will consume something valuable. Your visual marketing establishes an expectation in the viewer's mind. When done right, your consistent elements will let the viewer know that the content they're about to consume is worth their time and attention.

This adds to your overall brand perception.

Roles and responsibilities of visual marketers in a team

The way a visual marketing team is built depends on the size of your company. If you're a one-person wrecking crew, you have to wear many different hats. Creating the concept, writing the copy, designing, and then publishing the content can be a difficult job for a single person.

Larger organizations or organizations with budgets can afford to build a team with many people contributing to visual marketing. Ideally, you should have some mix of the following roles:

Creative director

This is the person who will help define the concept, provide direction, and ultimate creative approval.

Designer

Someone to establish the brand and create the ongoing visuals.

Brand strategist

This person considers the big picture of the brand. Are you telling the right story? This person knows what is needed and helps define and shape the overall brand.

Video producer

Someone to create and edit video concepts. This person could work alongside a sound designer.

Initiator

This could be a marketing manager, a director, a content manager, or someone else who is thinking about the prospect's needs and helping to initiate new projects. This role is usually outside the creative marketing team.

Copywriter

Visuals will only take you so far. You need someone to craft the message and write the copy to capture a prospect's attention. Sometimes, this person is also the Initiator.

Project manager

A lot goes into creating content. This role can ensure the projects are progressing and being delivered.

Distribution

Someone needs to post this great content somewhere. It could be on a blog, on YouTube, on social media, in an email, or elsewhere. This is an adjacent role that could be broken out into multiple roles.

The interdisciplinary approach to visual marketing, integrating design, strategy, and analytics

There is a difference between brand marketing and performance marketing. Brand marketing is a long-term strategy that builds positive sentiment in prospects and customers. Performance marketing is more focused on driving shorter-term measurable success.

When used together, brand and performance marketing power each other.

A brand is built up over time with every interaction the prospect/customer has with your business. You won't be happy with the results if you measure brand marketing after one interaction. The only way brand marketing happens quickly is when something has gone wrong. Getting buy-in on a plan will help prevent knee-jerk reactions if your marketing efforts aren't immediately performing.

When marketing technology (MarTech) systems are correctly connected, it is possible to measure the impact of content marketing on the bottom line. If someone visits your website, fills out a contact form to download a resource, and later purchases a product, you can credit part of that sale to the content they downloaded. This is why there is so much gated content out there. Marketers like to show why their expenses are essential to the company's growth.

The Lead Generation Process

Moving prospects to customers and beyond

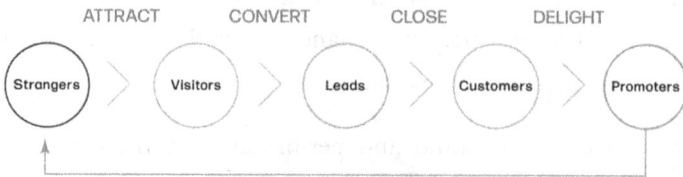

ATTRACT   CONVERT   CLOSE   DELIGHT

(Strangers) > (Visitors) > (Leads) > (Customers) > (Promoters)

Figure 2: the Lead Generation Process

Every contact added to your customer relationship management (CRM) system has potential financial value. Thinking of each email address as having a financial amount tied to it can reshape how you look at your content marketing. The visitor is giving/selling their email address in exchange for your content.

You better make that content worth it.

When your content is consistently well-designed and well-written, and your audience clearly understands the value they'll gain from it, that is the hallmark of strong branding. Aligning your content with your visual brand involves creating assets that people genuinely want because they're valuable. When your audience recognizes this value, they're more likely to share their contact information with you.

Case studies highlighting successful visual marketing campaigns

Many successful companies have run visual marketing campaigns and programs to bolster their branding efforts. Some of the best are so ubiquitous that you don't even realize that it was a marketing campaign.

Owens Corning was the first company to trademark a color.[2] Insulation is normally yellowish brown. However, due to a mistake where red dye was added to its product, Owens Corning decided to capitalize on this mistake and make it a differentiator.

In 1987, Owens Corning applied to the United States Patent and Trademark Office (USPTO) to own the color pink. This led to a 40-year relationship with the Pink Panther in its marketing efforts. What does an animated panther have in common with home insulation? Your guess is as good as mine. But they're both pink, and in this case, that's enough.

Budweiser is another company that excels in visual marketing. For almost a century, the Clydesdale has represented Budweiser in parades and other in-person events. They have featured prominently in advertising campaigns for nearly 40 years. These massive beasts' majesty helps promote Budweiser's slogan as the king of beers.

Figure 3: Photo by Jemima White on Unsplash

Budweiser also leans into the visuals of its bright red bowtie logo and classic brown bottle. The Budweiser red is almost on the level of awareness as the Coca-Cola red. Across sports sponsorships, bar signage, or in-store displays, the Budweiser color and wordmark are impossible to confuse with other beers on the shelf.

Its visual marketing never tries to be "edgy" or "cool." The Budweiser brand is constantly presented in a classic, upscale way, even though that may not be how the general public sees Budweiser. Even the sense of Americana surrounding much of Budweiser's marketing efforts runs counter to its origin (German) and ownership (Budweiser is brewed by AB InBev, a Belgium-Brazilian company). However, Budweiser has maintained its visual marketing themes despite the contradictions. It's a good case study for perception and reality not quite aligning.

Figure 4: iStock.com/bmcent1

Future trends in visual marketing and its growing significance

In the early 20th century, businesses relied on print advertising–newspapers, magazines, and billboards–to communicate their messages. Fast forward to the digital age, and marketers are now navigating a world where visuals need to stand out across websites, social media, email, and more. This shift, as well as future shifts, will require an understanding of the basics of design as well as the ability to adapt to new technologies.

Moving forward–both through this book and in the world at large–visual marketing will become more critical. Marketing is begrudgingly moving into a post-social media, post-SEO world as these become pay-for-play models. These platforms are evolving and becoming more expensive, where the brand with the deepest pockets can easily win. Brand building is one of the best ways to enhance marketing efforts and increase sales.

Visuals will continue to grow in importance because of the number of screens we're exposed to. There was a time when a movie used to be promoted with a single poster in a movie theater and a black-and-white ad in the local newspaper. Now, a movie can take over huge digital billboards in Times Square with combinations of motion and still graphics. The marketing for a major film can be an overwhelming experience now.

There are screens everywhere screaming for our attention. Consistent visuals tied to your marketing will help cut through the noise. Being consistent with those visuals and messages will help your audience jump the mental line to understanding what your brand means. While reading this book, there's a chance you're going to get tired of reading the word "consistent," but it's that important.

As visual marketing moves further into video and eventually the augmented reality/virtual reality/extended reality (AR/VR/XR) space, it becomes even more important to have a strong, consistent visual identity.

These are new spaces people are exploring for the first time. You must tie those new experiences back to the familiar experiences so they know you can be trusted in this new space.

People don't like new things. There's a reason pop songs repeat the chorus multiple times. When something is new, we have to create familiarity as quickly as possible. Using established visual elements in new environments helps speed up the process of moving the viewer from confusion to trusted familiarity.

In these new, disorienting environments, your consistent brand visuals are a beacon of trust they can rely on.

Your goal is to reach trusted familiarity as quickly as possible, no matter the environment. Consistent visual marketing is the express train to triggering a viewer's emotional bond with your brand. Once you've established consistency, you can start to play with the visual brand and be a little more flexible with creativity. It's about being innovative within the guidelines of the established visual brand. An established visual brand, used consistently, has a psychological impact on the viewer.

Visual Cues

- Visual marketing is more important than ever since we have so much competition for our attention.
- Visual marketing is about connecting your marketing messages with images, videos, and other visual assets to strengthen your brand.
- Visual marketing sits at the intersection of content marketing and brand marketing.
- Creative people always want to try new things and take chances.
- However, marketing is about presenting a consistent message to prospects and customers to build reputation and trust.
- If the visitor is giving their email address in exchange for your content, you better make that content worth it.

CHAPTER 2:

The Science of Seeing

"I dream in colour, and it's always very surreal."

— *John Lennon*

What catches your eye?

It's a simple question, but the answer varies from person to person. If we take a closer look, we'll start to see patterns emerge. While individual preferences vary, there are some universal principles that shape how we respond to visuals.

It boils down to the interplay between two forces: nature and nurture.

Nurture refers to the cultural influences we grow up with. Colors, symbols, and imagery can hold vastly different meanings depending on your background. In some cultures, white symbolizes peace and cleanliness; in others, it symbolizes mourning. These cultural factors shape how we interpret the visuals we encounter.

Nature, on the other hand, is controlled by biology. How we process images is hardwired into our brains. For example, our eyes are naturally drawn to areas of high contrast or motion. It's not something we consciously decide, it's simply how we're built to see.

Together, these two forces—what we learn from our environment and how the brain is wired—determine what grabs our attention and how we interpret what we see.

Figure 5: It's Science

How we consume visuals is based on science, and how we interpret them is based on culture. Your eyes ingest the visuals; those colors and shapes are sent to your brain; your brain reacts to what it sees.

Some reactions are subconscious. Like a clipped fingernail flying toward your eye, you will react without thinking. Believe it or not, there are aspects of visual marketing that also cause subconscious reactions.

Insights into human neuroscience and visual processing

By now, the following stat is well known: Humans process images 60,000 times faster than words. 3M conducted research to determine that we can understand image elements simultaneously, whereas words are comprehended following a linear, sequential methodology.[1]

In 2014, researchers at MIT discovered that people can identify an image as quickly as 13 milliseconds.[2] The researchers noticed that people were able to identify images that fast when given additional context ahead of time.

This boils down to simple science: Humans have been creating and interpreting images far longer than text.

If I showed you a photograph of an apple, you would know what it is right away. This also applies to an illustration of an apple and the logo for Apple Inc. However, when you read the word "apple," your brain has to consume all five letters, put them together to form a word, and then comprehend what those five letters represent.

Figure 6: Photo by Pixabay. Illustration by Rawpixel

It's fast, but it's not as fast as seeing a photo of an apple. Visuals allow us to understand concepts faster.

> *"...unless our words, concepts, ideas are hooked onto an image, they will go in one ear, sail through the brain, and go out the other ear. Words are processed by our short-term memory where we can only retain about 7 bits of information (plus or minus 2). This is why, by*

the way, we have 7-digit phone numbers. Images, on the other hand, go directly into long-term memory where they are indelibly etched."

—Dr. Lynell Burmark, Ph.D. Associate at the Thornburg Center for Professional Development.[1]

Humans have been creating and interpreting images for far longer than we've been creating and interpreting the written language. The earliest cave paintings are from 73,000 years ago.[3] The written language started only ~5,000 years ago.[4] We have been using images for nearly 70,000 years longer than words.

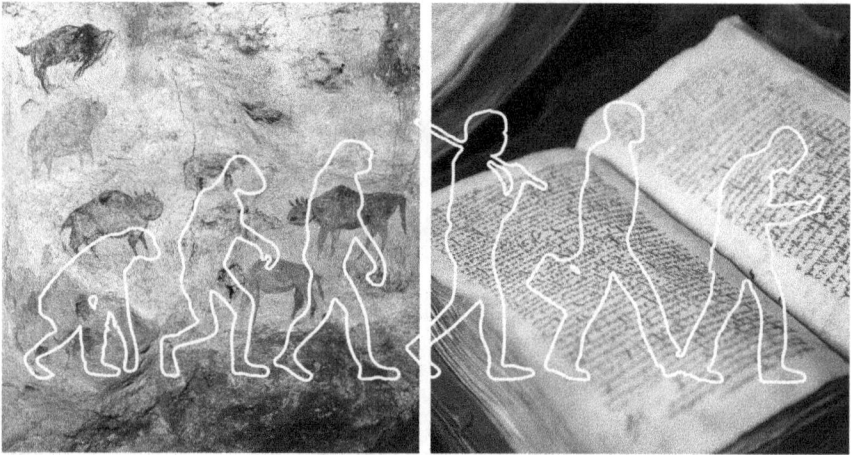

Figure 7: Midjourney prompts: "cave paintings" and "inside pages of a 12th century manuscript." Modified with Adobe Illustrator

The psychological impact of visuals on consumer behavior

All marketing comes down to trust. Trust is established through repeated interactions that meet or surpass expectations. Multiple factors

help build trust through numerous interactions. Visuals are a vital component to building that trust.

Visuals affect our emotions toward a particular brand. Different areas of
our brain are stimulated when presented with visuals that engage our creative thinking. The firing of these synapses leads to better comprehension,
retention, and recollection.[5]

When people are presented with visuals in marketing, it can lead to biological feedback based on the pre-existing feelings the person has toward
a brand. When presented with visuals of brands people didn't like, the
subjects were likelier to blink more often, had elevated skin conductance
(the measurement of the skin's electrical conductivity), and had increased
heart rate.[6]

When you see a brand, whether you like it or not, your body responds
instinctively—often in ways you may not even be aware of. It's an
automatic reaction.

Visuals influence both your psychological and biological states. Not only
can you better remember concepts when paired with visuals, but you feel
it ever so slightly across your body. Images can elicit engagement responses,
making you more likely to remember that information.

Visuals > emotions > greater recall[7]

You can better remember information with visuals because images have
more distinctive visual information than plain text. If this entire book was
just text, you wouldn't remember as much because every page would basically look the same. Luckily, you're reading a book about visual marketing,
so you'll see a bunch of visuals (makes sense, right?).

Statistics and research findings on visual content and decision-making

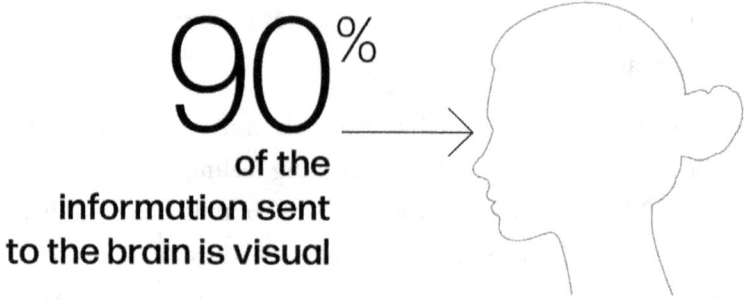

90%
of the
information sent
to the brain is visual

Figure 8: 90% of the information sent to the brain is visual

93%
of all
human interaction
is visual

Figure 9: 93% of all human interaction is visual

Articles with images get

94%

more views

Figure 10: Articles with images get 94% more views

Social media posts with images produc

150%

more engagement

Figure 11: Social media posts with images produce 150% more engagement

Visual content leads to

27%

higher click-through rates

Figure 12: Visual content leads to 27% higher click-through rates

Image searching is
estimated to be a

$40b

industry by 2025

Figure 13: Image searching is estimated to be a $40b industry by 2025

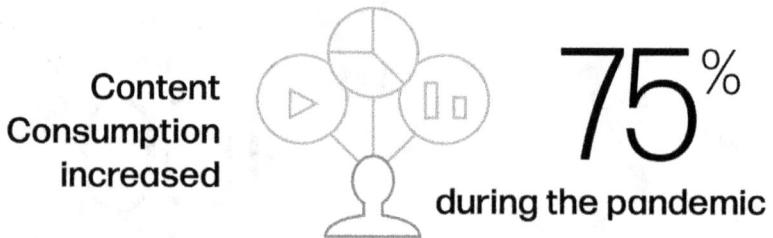

Content
Consumption
increased

75%

during the pandemic

Figure 14: Content consumption increased 75% during the pandemic

Videos can increase
conversion rates by

86%

Figure 15: Videos can increase conversion rates by 86%

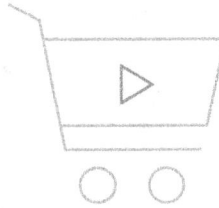

Shoppable videos convert
3x
more than traditional videos

Figure 16: Shoppable videos convert 3x more than traditional videos

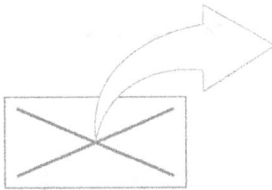

Visual content
40x
more likely to be shared on social media

Figure 17: Visual content is 40x more likely to be shared on social media

Memes can increase awareness by
60%

IT'S SCIENCE

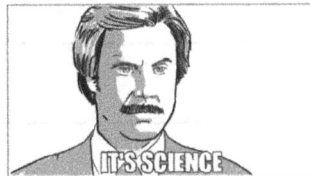

Figure 18: Memes can increase awareness by 60%

Facebook posts with images see

2.3x

more engagement

Figure 19: Facebook posts with images see 2.3x more engagement

The role of color, composition, and content in visual marketing

Color theory is essential when it comes to visual marketing. Specific colors evoke certain emotions from people and create associations based on previous experiences.

Many external factors (such as age, gender, and nationality) contribute to why people feel certain ways when they are presented with colors. Below is a chart that summarizes how people in Western societies tend to interpret different colors.

Color	Symbolic Meaning
Red	Stop, danger, anger, energy, action, passion, love
Orange	Energy, vitality, excitement, adventure, adventure, creativity, caution
Yellow	Happiness, joy, hope, optimism, creativity, energy
Green	Nature, peace, growth, luck, freshness, vitality, freedom
Blue	Trust, loyalty, authority, business

Color	Symbolic Meaning
Purple	Elegant, noble, romantic, and mysterious
Pink	Love, romance, femininity, childhood, nurturing
Black	High pressure, authority, low profile, despair, formal
White	Purity, peace, elegance, clean

I specifically noted Western society because colors have different meanings in different cultures. For example, in Western cultures, white tends to mean purity and is often used in bridal gowns. Meanwhile, in the East, white is associated with death. Chinese brides will often wear red as it's a color of good fortune. Since the West typically sees red as an aggressive, angry color, which means "stop", a red wedding dress may be considered a bad omen.

International Color Symbolism

	BLACK	WHITE	YELLOW	GREEN	BLUE	PURPLE	PINK	RED	ORANGE	BROWN
WESTERN										
EASTERN										
EUROPE										
MIDDLE EAST										
AFRICA										
CHINA										
INDIA										
THAILAND										
JAPAN										
Other	BRAZIL	ITALY / IRAN	IRAN	NORTH AFRICA	ITALY	ITALY	BELGIUM	ITALY	BRAZIL	BRAZIL

Figure 20: International Color Symbolism

Color guidelines are meant to be used as flexible frameworks. They are not rules or laws. For instance, a company can use green in its visual branding even if it isn't a nature-based business. There are no legal mandates when it comes to color interpretation. None of these guidelines are carved in stone. You can make generalizations, but at the end of the day, they're just guidelines, open to creative interpretation.

Guidelines, like rules, can be broken by those who understand the underlying theory. The adage "rules are meant to be broken" should be followed with "by those who understand the rules."

Some people view design and art as the same thing. It's not. Art doesn't have rules. Design does.

When someone knows the rules, they know how to break them. Without the basic underlying understanding, breaking the rules of design will be visible to everyone but you. You may not be able to see it, but your viewers will understand that something is "off."

Strategies for leveraging visual processing advantages in marketing

Knowing that people are attracted to visuals because of the simplicity in which they can be consumed and understood, marketers can find ways to use visuals to let the viewer know what they are about to consume.

Suppose I have a presentation with a robot on the first slide. In that case, there's a good chance the presentation will be related to technology, to robots, the Internet of Things, or Artificial Intelligence (AI). The viewer has been trained on the content likely tied to that image.

It's a shortcut. Using the right visual lets the viewer know what you're trying to say without forcing them to read the nine words in the title and subtitle(s).

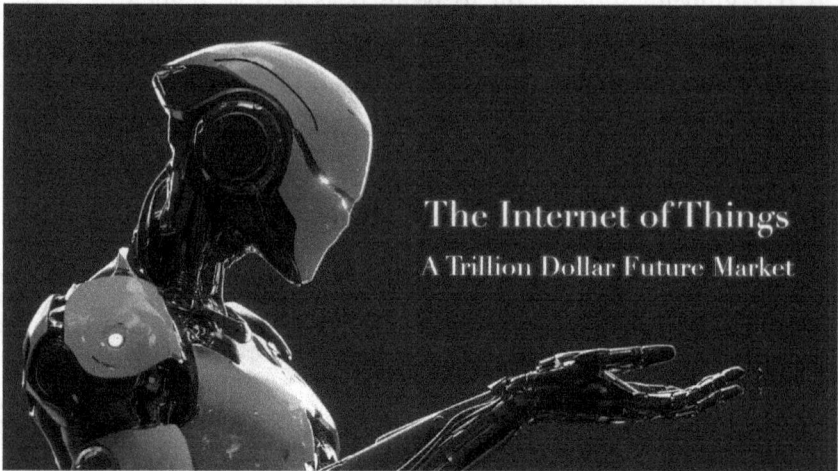

Figure 21: Midjourney prompt: a photo-realistic robot, in profile, holding out its hand

This image doesn't appeal to everybody, but it appeals to people who are looking for this type of content. Using known imagery–imagery that is generally understood by the public at large–means people who are skimming can recognize that there is content that may be interesting to them. It grabs their attention and forces them to slow down and read a little more.

This is why YouTube thumbnails are so important. As viewers look around the screen for the next video to watch, some thumbnails will stand out more than others. People are emotional creatures so the best thumbnails can fire emotional triggers. You want to tease the potential viewer with enough information to entice them to click and start watching.[8]

Faces

We're going to go deep on brain science for a few minutes, so I'll reward you with a cute dog photo at the end of this section.

We are biologically drawn to faces. It starts right after birth. Within the first few hours of life, babies are drawn to faces, particularly their mother's. Science has shown that the brain is wired to recognize faces as early as six days old. Using functional magnetic resonance imaging (fMRI) researchers have seen that baby's brains are set up to receive information about faces.[9] Studying faces is how babies start learning about the world around them.

There is a specific part of the brain, the fusiform gryrus, that responds to faces.[10] Research shows we're programmed to look at faces far more than other objects. Facial cues drive our understanding of the world around us.

> *"We all have mirror neurons—small transmitters in our brain that are responsible for adjusting our emotion to the emotional environment we find ourselves in. As an example, we feel happy when we see a smiling face, and this is an adaptive behavioural mechanism that has helped us to evolve as social creatures."*
>
> —*Binna Chopra, Research Manager at Spark Emotions*

Our brains recognize faces faster than any other object. This has been proven by fMRI studies that reveal that activity in the fusiform face area (FFA) of the brain lights up the most when the subject is looking at a face. This area lights up even when blind people are given face sculptures to touch. We use faces to identify people, identify emotions, and communicate with people.[11]

If you've ever wondered why we see faces when they're not there, it's because we're so wired to identify faces that our brains are more willing to misidentify something as a face than to miss a face.[12] This is a tendency called pareidolia. Faces tell us what is going on around us: Friend? Foe? Threat? Safety? We're always trying to answer these questions. It's biology.

Figure 22: iStock.com/Deagreez

Figure 23: iStock.com/Neal McNeil

Our attraction to faces has been measured by looking at eye-tracking heatmaps. Sometimes, photography of people is used to draw in the viewer so they can start to imagine themselves enjoying the product. Or it's a photo of something, like a baby, that will grab the prospect's attention.

Looking at eye-tracking heatmaps, you can see that the faces gather most of the attention on the page. The downside is that sometimes the viewer could be distracted by the faces and miss the call-to-action we want them to take.

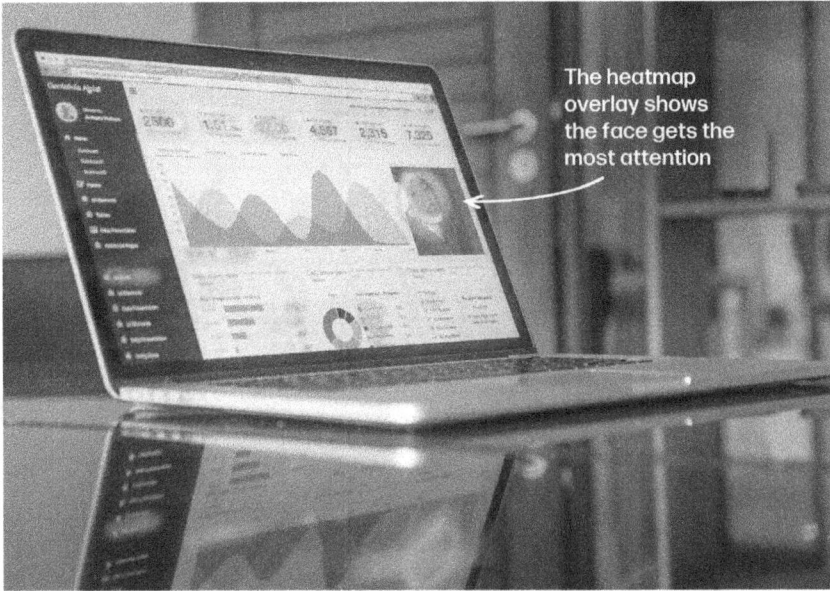

The heatmap overlay shows the face gets the most attention

Figure 24: Unsplash.com/Carlos Muza; modified in Photoshop

With this in mind, you can use the photos to help guide the viewer to the area you want them to see. Because viewers also follow eye gazes, you can design your ad or website to have the photo subject look at your call-to-action (CTA) area. The viewer will be drawn to the photo of a face and then follow the subject's eyes to see what they're looking at.

Science has also reinforced what we all know: people are more drawn to attractive faces. During the early developmental phases of life, babies are drawn to pretty faces because they tend to be more prototypical.[13] They better fit the ideal face that humans are innately drawn to.

> *"Our brains naturally look for patterns to learn from so we can make better decisions, and according to beauty standards and science, what makes a face attractive is symmetry. Symmetrical faces have more patterns than ones that aren't."*

> *—Juliana Stewart[14]*

Human faces work well, but we're not limited by species. Sometimes, an animal's face can drive a stronger emotional reaction.

Figure 25: This is Oliver, our rescued dachshund

We're hardwired to react to and feel similar emotions to those we're exposed to. What type of emotion do you want your viewers to feel?

If you're marketing a candy bar, you want the viewer to feel happy. Using photos of happy people enjoying the product is ideal. If you're selling life insurance, you may want the viewer to feel uneasy because they don't have enough life insurance. In this scenario, you'd want a photo of someone looking worried. These images will drive the emotions within the viewer.

It's a little bit manipulative.

Ethical considerations in visual marketing practices

Now that you understand the science behind how people react to visuals, you have to use this new power responsibly. Visual marketing can create ethical problems in a few ways: Exploitation, bait-and-switch, and Clickbait are ways that some people use visual marketing for less-than-scrupulous purposes.

Bait and switch tactics are often used in visual marketing. Think about the last time you were on an ad-supported news site. Many of those sites have links at the bottom that look like news stories, sometimes with a beautiful woman, to draw attention and get you to click to another less-than-good website.

Researchers have found that when mixed with an image, false information was more likely to be believed.[15] For example, if you had an image of a pig and a headline that read "Pigs are the only mammals that can't swim," it was more likely to be rated "True" even though nothing in the image gave that impression (pigs are excellent swimmers, by the way).

Figure 26: Midjourney prompt: photo of a pig standing on the dock of a lake; modified in Adobe Illustrator

People are emotional beings. Visuals can be used—both positively and negatively—to tap into those emotions and get the audience to take the action you want them to take. Visuals can be used on a slide to get an audience to remember a key takeaway, or they could be used to get someone to click on a link to a spam site (please don't do that; there's already enough spam in the world). Visuals can alter people's moods, even if they don't realize it is happening.

Now that you understand why people are drawn to visuals, it's time to learn how to use them to enhance your marketing efforts.

Visual Cues

- How we consume visuals is based on science; how we interpret them is based on culture.
- People can identify an image as quickly as 13 milliseconds.
- Humans have been using images for nearly 70,000 years longer than words.

- 93% of all human interaction is visual.
- Without the basic underlying understanding, breaking the rules of design will be visible to everyone but you.
- We are biologically drawn to faces.
- Visuals—both positive and negative—can be used to tap into emotions and motivate the audience to take the action you want them to take.

CHAPTER 3:

The Basics of Design

"Everything is designed. Few things are designed well."

—*Brian Reed*

Every piece of content should have a goal. If the viewer is not going to take an action, what do you want them to remember after viewing it?

Ideally, you want them to think of your business when it's time to solve their problem. To do this, you have to let them know:

- You understand the problem
- You can solve the problem
- You are the best option to solve the problem

You have a very short window of time to get these three pieces of information across.

Visual hierarchy and eye movement

When it comes to visual marketing, you must adhere to a set of width and height dimensions to convey all this information (plus attention-grabbing elements that we'll discuss later). Whether it's a banner ad or a trade show booth, you have a finite amount of space to answer the three challenges listed above. There are only so many pixels or inches available to get your message across.

It's your job to get the viewer to consume the content in the order you want. You would think that it's the way most people in the West consume content: Start in the upper left, move to the right, then down and to the left, then across to the right. This continues until they reach the end of the bottom right corner of the asset. We're taught to read in a z-shaped pattern (See Figure 28).

While that may be true in a book, it's not really how people consume visual marketing content.

Visual hierarchy will help the viewer easily determine which elements to view first, second, third, and so on. Using different focal points also makes it easier for their eyes to move around the asset.

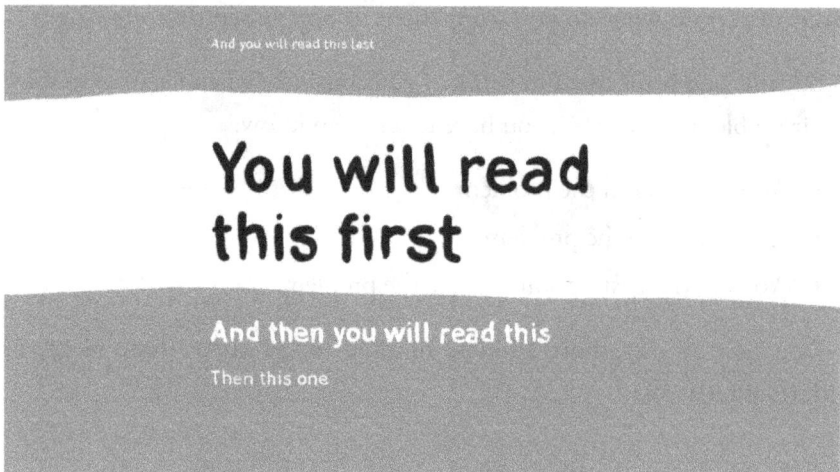

And you will read this last

You will read this first

And then you will read this

Then this one

Figure 27: You will read this last

This is the perfect example of visual hierarchy. I bet you didn't start at the upper left corner. You jumped right to the big, bold type in the middle and followed the text around just as it told you to.

To complicate things further, you probably noticed this as soon as you turned the page.

This works because we're drawn to information we can easily understand. The most prominent text with the most contrast is read first. The difference in colors between the headline and the background are further apart on the headline than on the lines on the gray background.

You have the ability to direct people to view elements in whatever order you want. You simply have to arrange the pieces in the right way.

Drawing the viewer in or getting them to stop scrolling is the first order of business. You have to have something that catches their eye. It could be a photo or some bold typography that gets them to focus on your visual marketing asset. Once you have their attention, you can guide them around the canvas.

This is where you want to demonstrate that you understand their problem. Whatever that problem, be it hunger, bad Wi-Fi, or a ride to the game, you must show that you understand it.

Then, you want to show that you can solve that problem. That could be a photo of a frustrated person who has yet to use your product. Or it could be a happy person who just used your product. The right visual will show that you can solve their problem. It's possible that these first two items can be achieved at the same time. But make sure you demonstrate both aspects: Show the problem; show the solution.

Finally, you want the viewer to mentally associate your brand with the solution to their problem. Logos are usually the easiest way to do this if you don't have a great-looking product.

Often, logos appear on an asset's upper left or lower right. If the viewer isn't captured by something big and bold in the middle, these are typically the entry (upper left) and exit (lower right) points. This helps establish the tie between your viewer's problem and the fact that you have the solution to that problem.

To confuse things further, there's nothing to say you can't put the logo in the upper right or lower left of the asset. Remember that you can move the viewer's eye around the asset, but people tend to move diagonally from upper left to lower right. This is why you see so many call-to-action buttons on the lower right of banner ads.

Figure 28: Unsplash.com/Austin Distel; modified in Photoshop

You want the viewer's eye to move around the asset so they can consume the key information as quickly as possible. Try to imagine a horribly impatient person. Now, imagine you're trying to sell them something. You only have a second or less to grab their attention and let them know they should buy from you.

Google's homepage is a prime example of a simplified visual hierarchy. The search bar is the focal point, placed centrally with minimal distractions. This forces users to pay attention to it and take the action Google wants: searching.

When it comes to the copy on your asset, people aren't going to stop and read a bunch of text. Get to the point and stop trying to be witty. Unless you're selling to marketers, witty copy doesn't have the effect you think it will. Keep it simple.

Once you have all of the elements, you have to establish a visual hierarchy so the viewer knows where to look.

You must have elements of different sizes and importance to have the viewer move their eyes around the canvas. If everything is large and bold, the viewer doesn't know where to look. Said another way: *if everything is yelling, you can't hear anything.*

 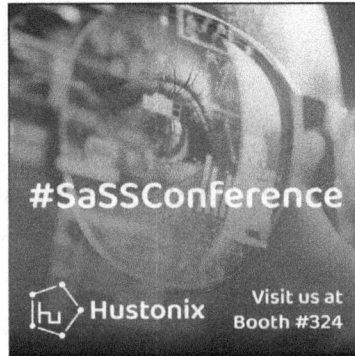

Figure 29A   Figure 29B

In Figure 29A, you can see how confusing it can be. What are you supposed to look at first? In Figure 29B, it's more obvious where the viewer should look first. Don't make it hard for the viewer to consume your content. The lack of separation between the text and the background image in Figure 29A creates more tension because it's hard to read the text on the busy background. There is also a bad tangent between the top of the logo and the frame of the eyeglasses. It's hard to tell what is going on. This lack of clarity and hierarchy will damage your brand. It looks amateurish and will be dismissed by viewers.

Figure 29A is also why "make the logo bigger" doesn't usually work. If one element—like the logo—starts to get bigger or bolder, it can ruin the visual hierarchy.

When you get a request to change the size of the elements, talking about visual hierarchy can help you change the mind of the person making the request (if they're wrong). Explain why a change can force the viewer's eye to jump around to different elements in the wrong order or in a way that doesn't follow their natural reading/consuming order.

The goal is to avoid visual tension. Visual tension is created when the viewer doesn't know where to look next. Their eyes are being pulled around the canvas in an unnatural order, which does the opposite of what you're trying to do. You want to enlighten the viewer, not confuse them.

Margins and the grid: Building a structured layout

When I'm reviewing a designer's portfolio, the first thing I look for is an understanding of "the grid." There is an invisible grid that sits under every design. Elements are arranged in special relation to each other and the overall canvas.

The grid establishes space and creates a sense of harmony across the canvas. When every element has its established space, the eye can move around the asset more freely.

Figure 30: Improper and proper grid alignment

Aligning elements to a grid avoids visual tension. There is a sense of disharmony when elements aren't properly aligned. This disharmony can create confusion and drive the viewer to leave your chaotic design because it takes more mental effort to understand what is happening. People don't like to look at chaos. They're already mentally taxed from the amount of visual information they take in every minute. They could move to the next thing if you add to this mental strain.

Even this book is designed on a grid. This page has invisible margins around the edges. From the top and bottom to the inside and outside margins, there is a visual balance to the page. Within those margins, there is a grid for each line and the space between the lines of text. The space before this paragraph is equal to the space after this paragraph. There is consistency in the spacing.

Because books are made of large blocks of text, the pages are smaller than your average piece of paper. This is because, at the end of each line, the eye has to travel all the way back to the left side of the page to go to the next line. It takes a little bit of unconscious effort to find the next line to read. If this book was printed at normal paper size, your eye would have to travel further back after each line. Finding the next line would be even harder if your eyes had to travel 10" rather than 6-7". Do this for every line across hundreds of pages and the viewer is going to get more tired than necessary.

The next time you think of making a text-heavy white paper on 8 ½ x 11" or A4 paper, remember not to use a full-width text block. Your audience will never finish it. You should have two columns or a text block that takes up 2/3 of the page. The extra third can be left blank with some minor visual element, or you can include a pull quote. Make sure it's visually different from the main body text because you don't want people reading that as the next line.

Figure 31: Example of white paper layout

As for margins, these help create breathing room around your elements. If elements touch the edge of your canvas, it could give the impression that there is more to be seen elsewhere. Using margins also prevents visual tangents. These are areas where a viewer's eye could start to move in the wrong direction at the wrong time. In Figure 32, you'll see how a bad tangent can create confusion. It's hard to tell where the table ends and the bowl begins. Once we add in text sitting right on the edge of the table and running into the apples, it creates more visual tension. We've now created an intersection between the table, the bowl, the apples, and the copy. The viewer won't instinctively know where to look next.

Another problem is the bowl is touching the edge of the frame. Points like this should either be away from the edge (like the image on the left) or cropped off. Don't have objects touching the edge of the image. It's an exit point and tells the viewer to stop looking at the composition.

Figure 32: Midjourney prompt: a photo of a bowl of apples on a table. Minimal background; modified in Photoshop

If you stick to the rule of thirds, you should be fine for aligning elements. When adding photography to a design, it helps to align the main subject with the invisible guides that put the main subject 1/3 of the way across the page. This is also why your smartphone has a 9-box grid when you're using your camera.

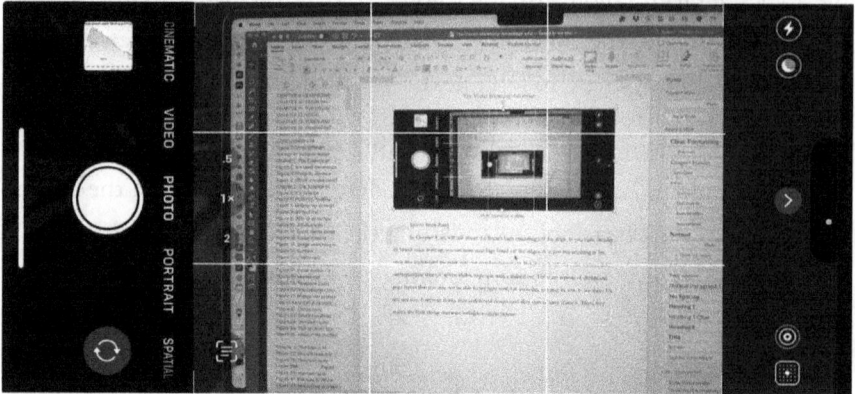

Figure 33: grid view on iPhone

"Today's users are constantly overwhelmed by content. With engagement times shrinking, standing out is more important than ever. Your imagery needs to reflect your brand's tone and quality, but it also must be tailored to the platform it's on. It's not enough to recycle a billboard design for Instagram—it simply won't work. Think about YouTube thumbnails: creators spend hours crafting them to make sure users know exactly what they're about to watch. All of this happens in a small, 720px canvas. That's the level of precision we need.

As designers and marketers, understanding photography is crucial. The principles of design still apply—particularly color, composition, and contrast. These elements can make or break your brand story. Contrast leads the eye through the image, whether through lighting, subject placement, or bokeh (lens blur). A quick tip: when editing images, start by working in black and white to nail down the right contrast, then focus on color.

Consistency in color ties your visuals together, while composition brings balance. The rule of thirds, for example, gives structure and harmony to your images, both vertically and horizontally.

Of course, not every marketer has the budget for high-end photography. Sometimes, you need a few more shots for a social ad, and time or money isn't on your side. In those moments, grab your phone! Modern smartphones can produce stunning photos with the right setup. Lighting is the key, and you don't need expensive gear to get it right. Even simple tools like lamps and printer paper can help you manipulate light to create something beautiful. Play around with bouncing light, shaping it, or adding texture—experiment and see what works.

This hands-on experience with light and composition will not only improve your immediate results but also help you communicate better with professional photographers in the future. It's all about understanding the basics and being resourceful."

—Alex Tourigny, Comercial Photographer
| UX and Motion Designer

In Chapter 4, we will talk about the Reese's logo extending off the edge of the canvas. If you have decades of brand value built up, you can have your logo bleed off the edges. Just like anything in life, once you understand the rules, you can start breaking them. But if you break the rules without fully understanding them, it will be visible to people with a trained eye. There are aspects of design and page layout that you may not be able to see right now, but someday, you may be able to. It's not just you. Everyone thinks they understand design until they start to learn about it. Then they realize the little things that were invisible to them before.

Take kerning for example. Kerning is the spacing between specific letters. You may have never thought about it before, but once you learn how to spot bad kerning, you'll always notice it.

No kerning

SAVE

Kerning applied

SAVE

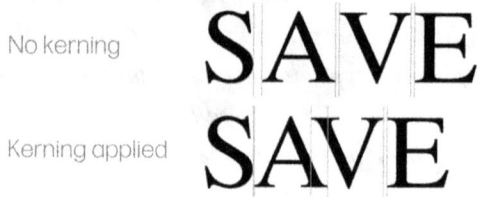

Figure 34: Kerning

A little trick for kerning, flip the text upside down. Your brain sees it differently because you start looking at it as shapes, not words. It's easier to see the space between letters when you think of them as shapes, and not as the word "SAVE."

Look at the space between letters

ƎVAS

Figure 35: Look for negative space between letters

Sometimes if you're not thoughtful with your kerning, other words can become visible, even if you didn't intend it.

Figure 36: Example of bad kerning

As the joke goes: if you hate someone, teach them about kerning because they will start to see bad kerning everywhere. But in this case, I don't hate you. I want to illustrate that there are aspects of design you haven't consciously thought about before.

(And sorry for introducing you to the nightmare that is kerning.)

Contrast to enhance visual impact

Because our brains process an incredible amount of visual information, they have to break down elements into their primary forms for fast understanding. This is a survival instinct honed over millions of years. High contrast helps us understand these elements faster.1 You noticed this in the "You will read this first" image (Figure 27) earlier in this chapter.

One of the reasons you noticed the "You will read this first" line first is because there is more visual contrast with that line than the other three. In black and white, it's easy to see the contrast difference between the "first" line and the others.

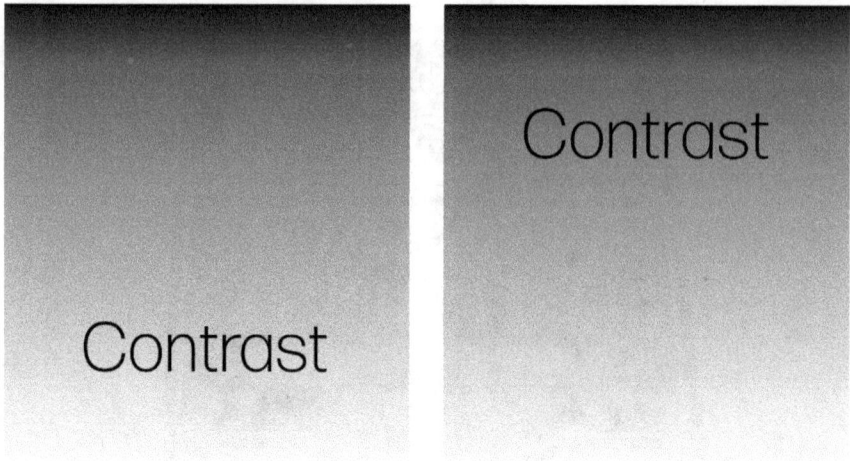

Figure 37: The more contrast, the easier it is to see and notice it

The cover of this book uses high contrast because I wanted you to see it. I wanted it to catch your eye, get you to pause, and learn more about the book. If you look at any streaming video platform, you'll notice that some thumbnails pop out more than others because of high contrast. Sometimes, you want to use similar colors to evoke a feeling, but that might not be the best way to attract initial attention.

One thing that helps with contrast is white space. By the way, white space doesn't have to be white; it just has to be empty (or negative) space around the elements. This helps create a border around your element. There are people (many of whom are in management positions) who hate white space. They see it as wasted space. But if they went to an art gallery, they'd notice a lot more white space than art.

Figure 38: Midjourney prompt: a photo of a wall from an art gallery. The wall is white with only two paintings on it.

White space helps focus the viewer's eye on the primary element. That's why we have frames around the photos on our walls or tables.

Fun trick: when framing an element, include a little extra space on the bottom. There is a visual weight that comes with a strong element. If that element is perfectly centered, it will look like it's a little too low. We have to create the illusion that the item is centered and account for the visual weight. Most photographs will have a frame that is a little thicker on the bottom because of this. Thanks to my 10th grade photography teacher, Bill Rapf, for teaching us this trick.

White space is your friend. Fight the urge to fill up all the space. The best design uses a ton of white space. It helps focus attention on the subject and allows the viewer to consume your content effortlessly. Lowering the level of effort helps with retention in both senses of the word. They'll consume your content for longer and are more likely to remember it.

One of the best parts of contrast is it also helps with accessibility. Accessible design means that visually impaired people have a better chance of viewing and understanding your visual marketing content. Accessibility is a form of inclusion. You want your content to be consumed by as many prospects as possible.

If you think back 10-15 years, creating responsive or mobile-friendly websites was the hot way to differentiate your business. Now, it's a given that your website is mobile friendly, if not simply mobile first. Accessibility is still in the differentiator phase. Soon it will be a given. Until then, make sure you're using the right levels of contrast with your design so visually challenged people can view your content.

As we saw in the Contrast image (Figure 37) a couple of pages ago, the copy is easier to read when the text color is further away on the color spectrum from the background color. You should consider this when designing because some people are visually impaired and need high contrast to read the copy. Multiple websites, including Acquia, accessiBe, and Deque, will check accessibility for you.

Putting it all together: Creating a banner ad

When you start assembling a piece of visual marketing content, it's like having the puzzle pieces but no box to use as a reference. Let's walk through the process of making a 250px x 250px banner ad.

Let's pretend we have a technology company called Hustonix that needs to run a digital ad to promote a new eBook you've produced. This company already has a logo and style guide that has mapped out the typefaces and colors you should use. As we'll discuss in later chapters, these guidelines not only help brand consistency but also make the creation of new content easier because you don't have to spend time on these aspects. There is also some pre-approved imagery you can use for this ad.

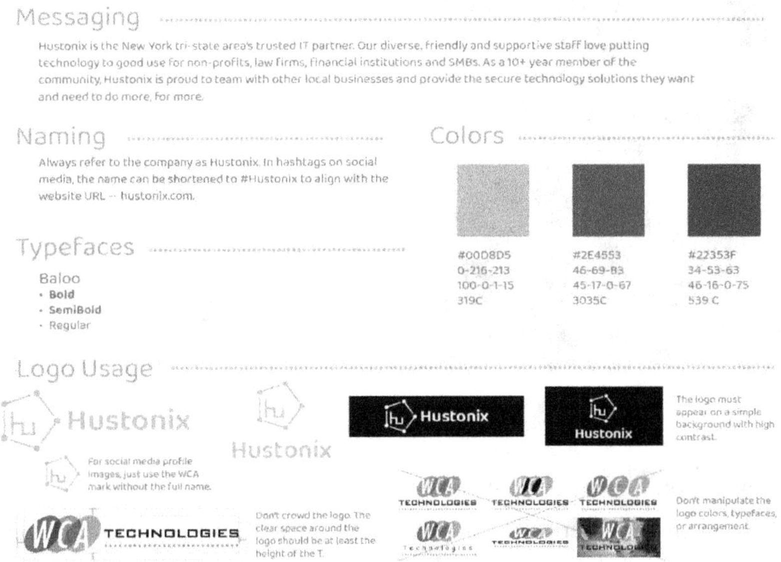

Figure 39: Page from Hustonix brand style guide

The eBook already has a title, but that may not be enough to draw the viewer in. Titles of assets and copy on an ad serve two different agendas. Sometimes the copy works for both, but if it doesn't, that's okay. The ad copy could come from several different sources (copywriter, product marketing manager, yourself, or someone else). Wherever it comes from, you already have it for this exercise.

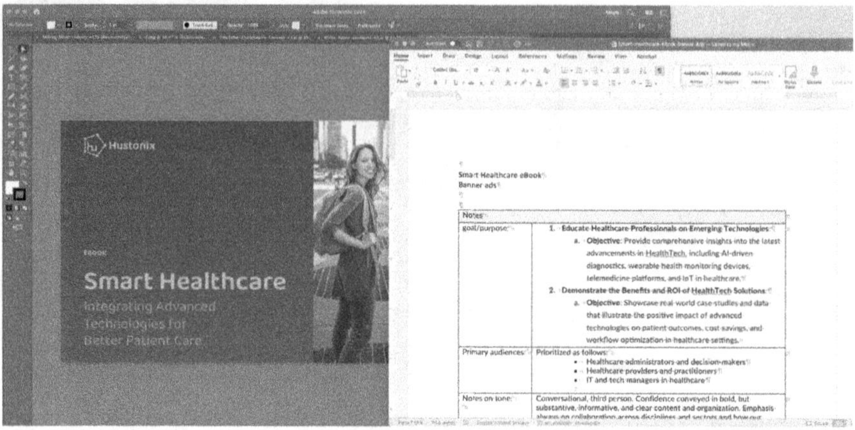

Figure 40: eBook design and copy deck

Finally, you'll need a call-to-action to get the viewer to take the action to click on the ad. Getting the viewer to fill out a form to read the eBook isn't the responsibility of this ad. Let's keep it simple. You want them to click on the ad to learn more about the eBook.

Now that you have all the pieces, you can start assembling the ad!

Let's start by drawing in some margin guidelines. This shows us where we need to keep important information. The copy, buttons, logos, and the key subject matter should reside within this box. General imagery can extend beyond the guidelines, but it shouldn't be anything important.

Figure 41: Start by adding guides for margins

In this case, the imagery—we're using a photo—should have less important areas. This allows you to add additional elements like copy, logo, and call to action.

This photo shows a woman looking directly at the viewer. Because we are drawn to faces and eyes (as discussed in Chapter 2), this photo works well to grab the viewer's attention. The main focal point of the photo is the woman's face, so it shouldn't be obstructed by any of the other elements.

You'll notice the woman's eyes sit close to the intersection of the rule-of-thirds guides we discussed earlier. I also blurred the background because this area is less important and I don't want people to notice it.

Figure 42: Photo added to canvas with guides

Once the photo is placed in, you can see we have even less real estate to work with. We have to be judicious with our other elements.

The headline can go around the middle because it helps balance the woman's face. Visual balance helps create harmony with the ad. The copy should stand out enough to be readable against the background. This is where contrast comes into play.

Because we're driving people to download an eBook, this is a performance campaign, not a brand campaign. We'll measure the number of people who click on the ad to learn more, so we'll put the call-to-action button in the lower right-hand corner.

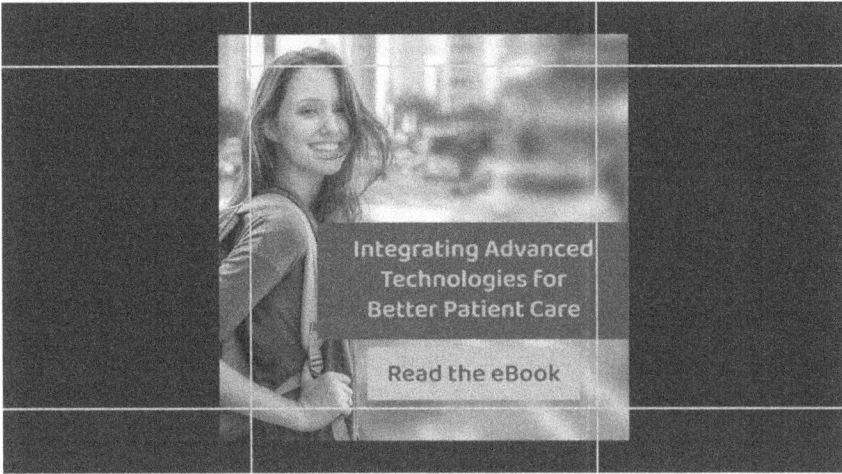

Figure 43: Add copy and visual elements

You're now seeing how the viewer's eye will move around the canvas. The woman's face captures the attention of the viewer. Then they look at the headline. Then they move to the call-to-action button. We can add additional elements that shouldn't distract from this 1-2-3 flow.

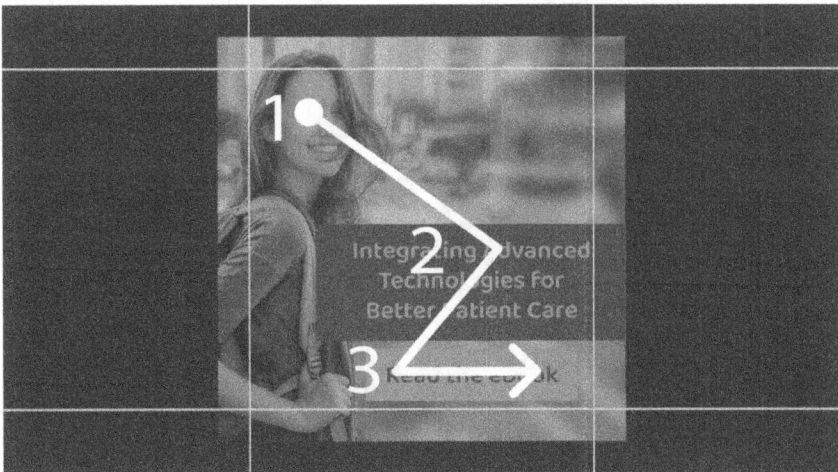

Figure 44: Consider how the eye will move around the ad

Another element that needs to be added is the company logo. Because this isn't a brand advertisement, the logo is less important than the other elements. You want people to know this ad is from your business, especially if you already have brand recognition. However, the primary responsibility of the ad is to get the person to click on it so they end up on your landing page.

In order to get the logo on here, but in a way that doesn't grab too much attention, I put the logo near the border. If it sat within the guides, it would attract too much attention. Pushing it close to the border indicates that it isn't as important. As we've established, the more space around an object, the more attention it commands. I also added a gradient behind the logo so it stands out from the busy background. There are times when you will want attention on your logo, but this isn't one of those instances.

I added a border to help establish a style that can be used across multiple ads. It helps anchor the dark box behind the headline. Connecting this box to the border helps make it more distinct from the free-floating call-to-action button. The bright button, with clear space around it, helps draw attention. The border connecting to the headline helps cement the visual hierarchy.

Figure 45: Leave room for the logo and any other brand-related elements

You could add additional information like a thumbnail of the eBook or a subhead to provide additional context. My recommendation for an ad this small is to keep it simple. In fairness, that's usually my recommendation for most things in life.

Now we can look at the ad and see if we need to move anything around or adjust the size of any elements. Figure 46 provides a few alternatives to show why making some elements larger doesn't help the overall ad. Your ad has to convey a sense of value to the viewer. Just posting your logo and a call-to-action to download an eBook won't drive someone to take the action you want.

In these examples, you can see how different elements fight each other for attention or pull your eye in unnatural directions. There are many ways to arrange these same basic elements. You'll be more successful if you're telling the right sequential story in this static ad.

Figure 46: Try different layouts

Finally, you should remember that this ad should be RGB. Digital displays are made of only three colors: red, green, and blue. Any other color you see is merely a combination of these colors.

If you were making a print ad, you'd want to work in CMYK. Cyan, magenta, yellow, and black are used to make up the rest of the printed color spectrum. This is why style guides will have multiple breakdowns for colors. One for RGB, one for CMYK, one for HEX (the code used to display colors on the web), and sometimes there will be Pantone color. This example just shows HEX, RGB, CMYK, and Pantone.

Colors

#00D8D5	#2E4553	#22353F
0-216-213	46-69-83	34-53-63
100-0-1-15	45-17-0-67	46-16-0-75
319C	3035C	539 C

Figure 47: Brand colors have hex, RGB, CMYK, and Pantone designations

Ever notice how you print something at home and the colors aren't quite right? The Pantone Matching System (PMS) is the universal standard for colors. When you provide the PMS number, any professional printer can match and print the same color. FYI: The printer in your home or office is not a professional printer. Those printers just print CMYK.

If you request a printed item to use Hustonix's teal Pantone color, PMS 319C, every professional printer will be able to match that color. Sometimes you'll see a second PMS color that ends in a U. Colors print differently based on the material they're printed on. The C stands for coated and the U stands for uncoated material.

These are just the high-level basics of design. Design is a discipline that contains infinite learning. There's no way a book, let alone a single chapter, can fully train you to be a designer. I hope these previous few pages help get you started in the right direction. It's hard to go wrong when you keep things simple.

By simple, I mean never use more than two typefaces and keep your color palette to just two or three colors. If you start using every typeface, effect, and color, it will look unprofessional. Your viewers don't want to see how cool you can make it; they want to see the information that pertains to them.

> *"Perfection is achieved not when there is nothing more to add, but when there is nothing left to take away."*
>
> *—Antoine De Saint-Exupery*

Visual Cues

- Your goal is to be top-of-mind when someone has a problem to solve.
- We're drawn to information we can easily understand.
- You have the ability to get people to view elements in whatever order you want.
- Keep your visual hierarchy simple.
- Imagine you're trying to grab the attention of a horribly impatient person.

- Visual tension is created when the viewer doesn't know where to look next.
- There is an invisible grid behind every piece of content that establishes space and creates a sense of harmony across the canvas.
- The rule of thirds says to align essential objects on the 1/3 lines (part of the invisible grid).
- Kerning is the space between letters. Flip the text upside down to better see kerning that might be "off."
- White space helps focus the viewer's eye on the primary element.
- Visual contrast (colors, size, or white space) helps with catching attention and accessibility.

CHAPTER 4:

Crafting Your Visual Value Proposition

"Price is what you pay. Value is what you get."

—*Warren Buffett*

A value proposition is a way to show the benefits a prospect will experience if they buy your product or service. You have the best product or service, right? Well, how do you demonstrate that to prospects?

You have to find a way to differentiate what you do from what your competition does. Illustrating these differences can be the difference between closing the sale or losing it. Otherwise, you get lost in a sea of sameness. Looking like your competition doesn't help you stand out. You need to outline why a customer should choose your product or service.

Take Warby Parker, for example. Their visuals consistently reflect simplicity, accessibility, and style. From their website to their Instagram feed to their physical stores, Warby Parker's minimalist aesthetic communicates their promise of affordable luxury and smart fashion.

Steve Blank—the entrepreneur who established the lean startup movement, a methodology that explains that startups need to be run differently than corporations—uses the simple formula "We help (X) do (Y) by doing (Z)."

Identifying and defining your brand's unique visual value proposition

Now that we've clarified a value proposition, the next question you're probably asking is, "What is a visual value proposition?"

Adding visuals to a value proposition helps simplify its complexity (though Blank's formula is very simple) and delivers it uniquely. Using images, photos, and other iconography to communicate the message can be a shortcut to the viewer's understanding.

The difference is the medium. Using visuals versus the written word helps people understand the message more easily and remember it for longer. Images are more likely to be remembered than text. The Picture Superiority Effect demonstrates that information presented with visuals leads to recalling 65% of the information three days later, compared with recalling just 10% after three days when it is just text or audio.[1]

The Picture Superiority Effect

Amount of information recalled after three days

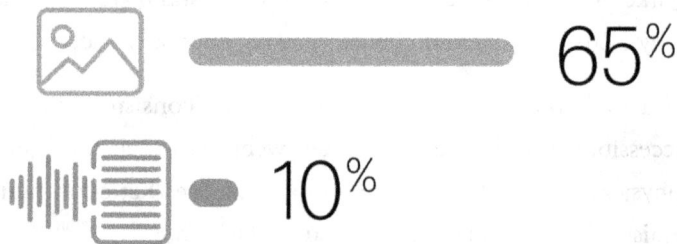

65%

10%

Figure 48: People retain more information from seeing than hearing or reading

When you're getting prospects to know, like, and trust you—a foundational concept of content marketing coined by Joe Pulizzi, founder of the Content Marketing Institute—being top of mind is essential. Visuals are a powerful tool in achieving this because they create stronger, more memorable impressions compared to text alone. When a prospect or potential customer encounters a problem, you want your solution to be the first one they think of.

One of the reasons visuals resonate deeper is that the viewer can tie an emotion to the message. It's much easier to correlate an emotion to an image than the written word. In our fast-paced, noisy world, we're bombarded with words and imagery pushing messages at us. The right visuals can offer nuance that sentences or paragraphs can't. In Chapter 8, we'll dig into how to build out your visual brand.

Techniques for aligning visual content with brand identity

As you create your brand identity, you want to make sure your visuals align with the message you're trying to tell. People don't buy medical devices if the packaging looks like a preschool coloring set. These visuals must appeal to your prospective audience.

Let's say you're opening a new doggy daycare. Your audience is made of people who love their dogs but need someone to watch and care for them for a while during the day. Or, their dogs may be rambunctious like mine and need to burn off some energy with friends.

The visuals for a business like this need to find the right mix of playful and caring. More often than not, this business would use photographs of dogs playing and having a good time. The owners need to know that their beloved four-legged friends are going somewhere they'll enjoy. This is where emotion comes into play.

There is a baseline of fear associated with handing over their best friend to a stranger. Potential customers need to feel that their dogs will be okay.

One of the best ways to get prospects to trust you is with visuals that show you know what you're doing. The right mix of warm imagery, playful typography, and the right copy, can help establish that you can be trusted to care for their pets.

Strategies for differentiating your visual content in a crowded market

Like starting a business, you must find white space in a market. Finding an area of need that hasn't been filled yet is where you can differentiate your business.

This applies to visuals, too.

Start by taking inventory of your competitors' activities. Are they using photos? What colors are being used or owned by competitors? Are they using humor? How much copy are they using? These are all good questions to start asking. Asking these and other questions will allow you to see patterns, and then you'll start to identify areas that are open and appeal to potential customers.

Color is a great way to stand out. When it comes to technology companies, many use blue because it symbolizes trust and security. Intel, Dell, Meta, Cisco, HP, GE, Salesforce, Samsung, and even big blue itself, IBM, have built their visual brands on the color of trust.

If you were looking to compete against any of these companies, you'd want to go in the opposite direction. Oracle, Xerox, Alphabet, YouTube, Netflix, and others in the technology space have gone all-in on using red.

In many industries, the two leaders tend to split between red and blue: Coke/Pepsi, CNN/Fox News, Marvel/DC, Red Sox/Yankees, Target/Walmart, Republicans/Democrats, Budweiser/Bud Light, Netflix/Disney+, the list goes on and on.

Starting to see a trend?

If the dominant player in your space is one of these primary colors, go in the opposite direction. If the market is saturated with companies using these two colors, go in a completely different direction. There are a lot of colors out there.

The same applies to the type of visuals you use. Let's say you're in the car rental space. If all the major players use high-end photography, you could differentiate by creating eye-catching graphics using simplified shapes. Finding or creating cutting-edge graphics would help the prospect understand that your car rentals aren't the same as everyone else's.

This isn't a situation where you can just use a simple Canva template. The graphics must look high-end because you're selling access to a vehicle that costs thousands of dollars. If the graphics look cheap or low effort, viewers will assume the cars you offer are also cheap.

Your visuals must be different in a good way. This won't always be obvious when you're starting. But as time goes on and you see how different visuals perform, you'll better understand what works and what doesn't.

The role of storytelling in enhancing your visual value proposition

The visuals you create should allow the viewers to picture themselves as part of that experience. There is a storytelling component to visuals, even when they are static.

One of the reasons why so much stock photography shows a range of ethnicities, ages, and genders is because you want your target audience, no matter what demographic(s) they fall into, to feel as though they can see themselves having the experience you're selling.

Be careful not to overuse stock photography. A 2023 survey of marketers showed that stock photography performed worse than any of their other visual content.[2] (Original graphics performed the best, by the way).

These people are coming to you because they have a problem and hope you can solve it. No matter the problem–broken car, acne, thirst, or vacation planning–you're selling the benefit that is the result of using your product or service.

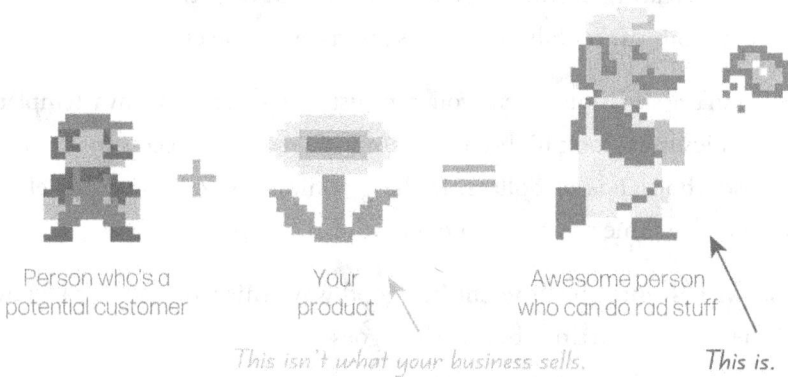

Person who's a potential customer | Your product | Awesome person who can do rad stuff

This isn't what your business sells.   *This is.*

Figure 49: 2013 UserOnboard.com

The benefit or end result of what you're selling needs to be shown in your visuals. As UserOnboard.com wrote, "People don't buy products; they buy better versions of themselves." Every single person is the lead character in their story. They're on a journey, and your product's job is to help them achieve their wins.

> *Your visuals can help them envision achieving their goals. The difference between where they are and where they want to be is your product or service.*

Michelob Ultra does this with its visuals. Looking at their marketing makes you forget they're selling beer. Their ads are full of fit people who have just finished working out and are ready to reward themselves. The low-calorie/low-carbohydrate beer is practically marketed as a health drink. Go run five miles and enjoy a Mic Ultra. You've earned it, and you'll feel better. Really?

The visuals of a Michelob Ultra ad today and a Gatorade ad from ten years ago aren't significantly different.

Michelob tells a story that appeals to people who want to be healthier but still want to drink beer. Its visuals reinforce this because they show people who are the idealized state for this target audience.

We help (X) do (Y) by doing (Z).

We help (beer drinkers) (be healthier) by (drinking Michelob Ultra).

or

We help (healthy people) (enjoy beer) by (drinking Michelob Ultra).

This helps Michelob Ultra appeal to two audiences by telling a similar story.

Examples of brands with strong visual value propositions

Spotify is another company that worked hard to create a visual identity that portrayed its value proposition. Even though it is an audio service, in the early days of Spotify, the Swedish company used very strong visuals to communicate what it stood for. Using a consistent duo-tone effect on visuals within its marketing and in-app experience helped establish Spotify's presence in the U.S.

The photos looked different than anything else on the market at the time. It signified that this was a new type of music service. It was something that forced you to pay attention. Add to that a neon-green logo that looks like sound waves, and you couldn't help but notice.

The duotone treatment that was applied to the photos was so popular that it is now called the Spotify effect. If you ask any designer, it's the easiest treatment to apply to a photo. It replaces all the color with just two colors and the range of colors between those two. In the picture below, the blacks are magenta, the lights are yellow, and everything else falls between those two colors.

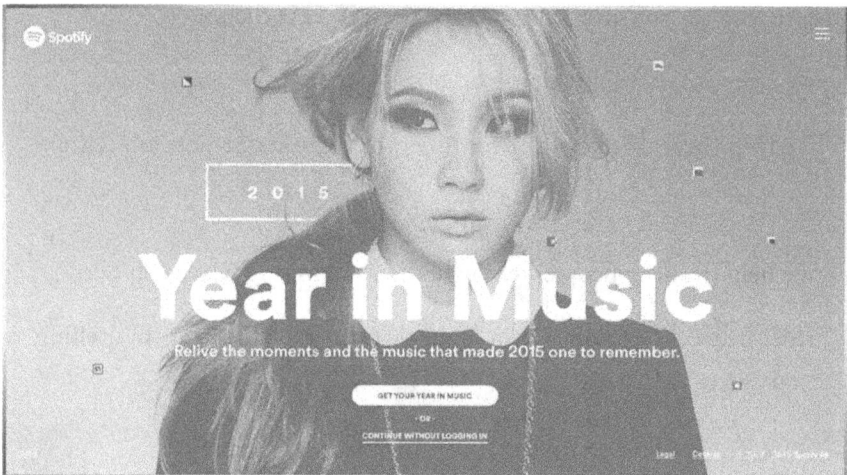

Figure 50: Early Spotify Wrapped

Reese's is another brand with great visuals that leave no doubt what they're selling. In consumer goods, unlike B2B products or services, showing the product helps market it.

Reese's is one of those companies that "owns" its color. We'll get more into this concept in Chapter 8. When you see that flat orange, you know it's a Reese's ad. The fact that these ads can crop the logo shows how much brand equity the name and logo have. Usually it's a big no-no to crop a logo, but Reese's gets away with it because of decades of consistent visual branding. Between its marketing and its products, that yellow and black script logo on an orange background reminds people of the happiness that comes with a Reese's Peanut Butter Cup or a handful of Reese's Pieces.

Reese's can be cute with its copy because, more likely than not, whoever is viewing its visuals has experienced its product at one point or another. Reese's isn't worried about building brand awareness. It's focused on staying top of mind. It can be a reminder that you want a snack and a Reese's Peanut Butter Cup would taste great right now (I know I want one), or the next time you're feeling snacky, you might be more likely to remember the ad and reach for that delicious mixture of chocolate and peanut butter.

Figure 51: Reese's bold visual branding

Tools and resources for brainstorming and defining your visual value proposition

When done right, brainstorming can be a great source of ideas and a lot of fun. No idea is too outlandish—anything goes. Sometimes, the worst ideas turn out to be the answers the group sought.

Some brainstorming sessions can also be good times for research. Having someone who can quickly search when a new idea arises can be a powerful advantage.

You'll first want to search for competitors in your space to see what they're doing from a visual standpoint. Moat.com used to be a great site that showed hundreds of digital ads from thousands of companies. Unfortunately, its new owner changed it to a different type of site.

Facebook's ad library is a decent replacement because it shows a variety of ads, the dates they ran, and the platforms upon which they ran. One drawback is that, because Meta properties boost video content over static content, most ads are video, so they take longer to review.

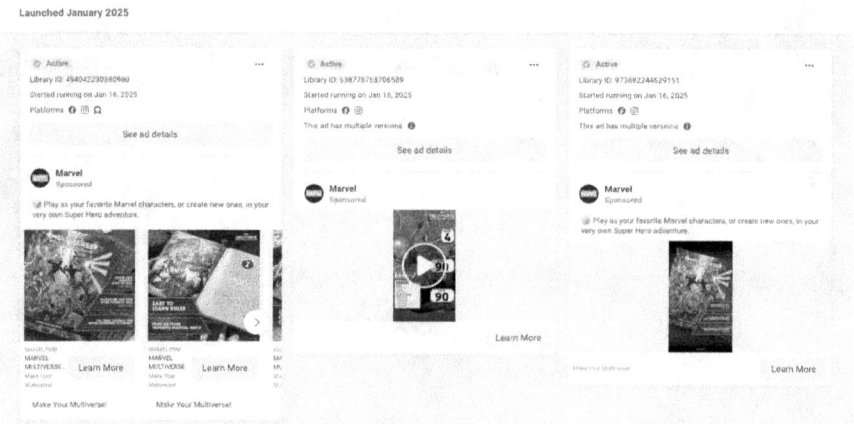

Figure 52: Screenshot of Facebook ads

Paid platforms, including Semrush, Similarweb, and HubSpot Marketing Hub, can help. These options will give you additional information, such as the traffic and performance volume of the ads. Some are focused on search ads, whereas others give information about paid social.

Once you've evaluated the competitive landscape, you can start to identify trends. Miro is a good tool for gathering and posting images. If you want to save a few steps, set up Pinterest boards based on your competition. When you can zoom out and see many of their ads at once, you'll notice key aspects of the visuals, namely colors, image types, text treatment, and copy volume.

Knowing your competitors' visual habits will show you areas where you can differentiate.

Once you've identified how to stand out and differentiate yourself, you can start creating your visual value proposition. If you don't have design skills, you can create mood boards or swipe files of visuals you like from companies outside of your industry segment. If you're going to work with a professional designer, aiming them in the right direction will save you time and money.

I highly advise against using pre-designed logo sites. They're grossly unoriginal, and the same design has likely been sold to other companies. You might be able to find a cheap designer on Fiverr or 99 Designs, but you don't want that. Establishing this part of your business is worth more than a hundred dollars. These should only be used if you treat the deliverables as mood board inspiration.

Canva can provide some inspiration, if you know that anything created in Canva is available to anyone else. It's impossible to stand out if everyone uses the same ingredients to create visuals. The same applies to generative artificial intelligence.

Also, if you use a pre-designed logo from Canva, know that you don't own it. You can't trademark it. Canva owns the rights to that design. Plus, anyone else can use it for their business.[3]

Caveat emptor for low-cost, high-output tools or services. You get what you pay for.

Thinking about your audience and what will appeal to them will guide you toward a logo that attracts the right prospects. There's a good chance your competition has already done a good amount of the work to determine what will appeal to your potential audience. Learn from their successes and failures.

Visual Cues

- You have to find a way to differentiate what you do visually from what your competition does.
- The Picture Superiority Effect demonstrates that information presented with visuals leads to recalling 65% of the information three days later, compared with recalling just 10% after three days when it is just text or audio.
- Visuals resonate deeper with the viewer because it's easier to tie an emotion to the message.
- In many industries, the two leaders tend to split between red and blue.
- There is a storytelling component to visuals, even when they are static.
- "People don't buy products; they buy better versions of themselves."

CHAPTER 5:

Understanding Your Audience

"Talk to your customers."

—Every lazy marketing "thought leader" on social media

Understanding what makes your business unique is important. Understanding your audience is critical. Understanding their motivations will not only help you shape your messaging, but it can also help you shape your offerings.

"Talk to your customers" is an obvious statement that is unfortunately ignored by businesses that never seem to understand why their business isn't more successful. Understanding your customers and prospects will tell you what and how to sell your product or service.

Understanding your audience can best be exemplified by digital platforms run by algorithms. These systems track a user's activity and then feed more content that is likely to be consumed by that person. Find out what they want and give them more of that!

Opening lines of communication with customers and prospects helps establish and build trust. Many large companies have customer-advisory boards (CABs). These are focus groups that meet regularly to help inform the direction of the products or services that the business is making.

Trust and a feeling of inclusion will strengthen customer and business bonds. And since you're building products or services they've influenced, they're more likely to help promote those offerings because they feel a sense of pride and ownership.

Techniques for creating detailed buyer personas for your visual content

Buyer personas go one of two ways: They're created and ignored, or they help shape your future marketing efforts.

Sometimes, the senior leadership has added someone new who swears by buyer personas. This leads to the team spending hours/days/weeks/months creating them. Everyone looks at them once, and the PPT files are then stored on an internal server somewhere to collect digital dust.

This isn't always the case, but it's been known to happen.

Defining personas can be a highly useful process if the outcome is something that the sales and marketing teams will use. These are most useful when the buyers are grouped into a few personas. I once saw a company that had 19 personas for one vertical. If you multiply this across 5-6 verticals, your persona work becomes useless. It's borderline impossible to market to 100 different personas. It could be possible, but I have yet to work for a company with an unlimited marketing budget.

If you don't have the time or money for infinite budgets, I prefer to focus on a few key audiences. One of those audiences should be your ideal customer. Another should be the person most likely to discover your offerings.

It's also important to recognize that who you **want** to reach and who you **can** reach are often two different personas. Of course, everyone's life is easier if you can market directly to the decision maker (AKA the person who controls the budget decisions), but the reality is your entry point is probably further down the chain of command. Tailor your content to empower this person to make the case within their organization that your product/service is the best option.

Early in the buyers' journey, you want high-level, top-of-funnel content. Visual content is most important here. This content lets the prospect know that you understand their problem and have a solution.

At this point in the buyer process, the prospect is identifying the problem and potential vendors. They are still skimming. Visual content, like infographics or short videos, are a great way to get the message across because they are fast and easy to consume.

Analyzing and interpreting audience data to tailor visual content

There is a ton of data available for your target audiences; it all comes down to how much you want to work (or pay) to access it. Only invest the time and money for this research if it's going to inform your marketing efforts. Some senior leaders trust their gut over data. Knowing this will save you time and frustration.

Data is only useful when it's analyzed, understood, and acted upon.

Since this is a book about visual marketing, it makes sense to find a way to visualize the data you're investigating. There are multiple dashboard tools out there like Qlik, Looker, or the industry leader, Tableau. These systems ingest data from multiple sources and give you an overview. Many of these are enterprise-level tools that require a significant amount of up-front work before they're valuable.

Once you have a literal view into your audience data, you'll better understand your target audience. Once you know them, you'll be able to create visuals that will engage them.

For younger audiences, vibrant and bold visuals can be more attractive. Older audiences tend to respond more favorably to refined, classic, and subdued color palettes. But these are just guidelines, not hard and fast rules.

Spotify Wrapped is an annual campaign that uses automation to create custom experiences for every Spotify subscriber. Because the visuals are based on the subscriber's listening history, subscribers feel special and want to share their Wrapped reports with their friends, family, and fans. It's a great way for Spotify to use graphics to get attention for its product because its customers are promoting their Spotify Wrapped results for all to see, leading to increased shares and engagement across platforms.

The importance of demographic, psychographic, and behavioral data in content customization

Knowing who could be interested in your product or service, how they think, and how they act, can help shape the visual content you're creating. It is a cliché to say, "talk to your customers," but understanding who they are and what motivates them will help you craft content that will get them to take the action you want them to take.

An easy way to differentiate these ways to measure and categorize people:

- **Demographic:** this is statistical data including age, gender, ethnicity, and location
- **Psychographic:** this helps you understand the attitudes, aspirations, interests, values, and personality traits
- **Behavioral:** this is how people act, including purchase history, brand loyalty, and response to marketing activities

While demographic data tells you who your audience is, psychographic data reveals why they make decisions. Understanding both gives marketers an advantage to craft visuals that resonate on a deeper level, aligning with their audience's motivations.

Basic demographic information, such as age, location, or gender, can help define the types of visual content you're creating. As we discussed in Chapter 2, if your audience is located in different parts of the world, you have to be careful with the colors you use. You don't want your fun ad to be interpreted as being associated with death.

Psychographic information can be harder to get.

Psychographic data will let you understand why people do what they do. Knowing their aspirations and interests will reveal the motivation behind their behavior. If you discover a prospect is looking for a promotion, your visuals should be aspirational; let them envision themselves as the hero saving the day.

There is a chance that many of your personas will have similar secondary interests that you can promote to show you understand them. For example, if your prospect collects vinyl, there is a chance they like to see concerts or play an instrument. Your visuals could help them envision being at a concert, or, even better, being up on stage!

Finally, behavioral stats will show what your prospect actually does. In the digital space, this is the easiest data to get, even with the decline of third-party cookies. Did they open that email? Did they visit that web page? Did they click on an ad? You might not know exactly who did what, but you'll have enough data to give you a general understanding of how a particular persona behaves.

As AI expands its capabilities across marketing technology systems, testing creative is getting easier. For years, Google has been automatically serving up the best-performing ad creative. It has been running the tests for you. All you have to do is upload different variations to be tested.

Tools and platforms for audience research and analysis

We've already talked about dashboard tools. But what about the systems that feed those dashboards? Account-based marketing platforms like 6sense and Demandbase have grown in popularity because those systems offer insights into your target audience and their behaviors. Knowing what they're doing and where they're doing it can help shape the type of visual content you create and what should be included. If they're spending a lot of time on TikTok, you'll want content that fits the rest of their feed. This could be fun, silly video content to make the viewer laugh. If they pay for high-end news, the banner ads you run should probably be more sophisticated than your TikTok content. But even differentiating "fun" or "sophisticated" should be determined by a combination of the audience and the platform.

Other systems, like Google Analytics, will provide some high-level data on the visitors to your website and/or apps. Knowing this information will help you identify the audience which will inform what type of content you should create.

A recent addition to the audience identification space is SparkToro. Co-created by the original co-founder of MOZ, Rand Fishkin, SparkToro allows people and businesses to do audience research. Discovering what actions your audience does around the internet can help define the audience. Creating data-backed personas is so much better than listening to the most tenured salesperson who has been farming the same key accounts for ten years.

Strategies for testing and refining visual content based on audience feedback

In addition to Google Ads, there are other ways to test and refine visual content.

I am a big fan of testing and measuring (don't forget the measuring part!). Try the same email with different visuals. Your email service probably allows for A/B testing. Do the same with content you post on different social platforms.

Make sure you limit your tests to one variable at a time. When testing visuals, make sure the copy is the same and it's deploying at the same time or being shared on the same site. When measuring visual in a test, prevent any other variables from skewing results.

If you're going to do A/B testing, make sure you measure the results and take actions with that new information. It takes a lot of time to set up a testing plan. It should take just as long to measure and implement the information you glean from it.

Focus groups are another area where you can gather valuable audience feedback. Asking simple questions can start the conversation. Then dig deeper. It's important to discover *why* they feel the way they do.

Years ago, I returned to my alma mater and had the opportunity to participate in a design critique. The professor (whom I didn't have when I was there) had a clicker in his hand. He clicked it whenever someone used the word "like." Whether someone likes or doesn't like something is useless information when critiquing a design. The design has a job to do, and the critique should be focused on whether that piece did the job or not. This is the same reason why the first round of a logo design project is usually in black and white. The designer is looking for the best design, not whether you or the client will pick the orange over the purple.

It's your job to identify the subject's personal preference, throw it out, and dig deeper to discover why they have that preference. Keep asking why to discover the real reason.

User surveys and feedback can be useful if you don't have direct access to a focus group. Make sure you phrase your questions in a way that doesn't bias the answers (for example, "Why do you love this poster?"), but avoid personal preferences getting in there and clouding the data.

On the digital side, multiple strategies exist, such as monitoring engagement across your owned properties and third-party properties. Analytics tools can give you an idea of what visuals resonate with the audience you're targeting. Tools like Optimizely or VWO allow you to easily run A/B tests on your website.

Your users will tell you what they want. You just have to listen.

When Electronic Arts (EA) was rolling out a new version of SimCity, it ran an A/B test that surprised everyone involved. They offered two versions of the main page for the game. The control version was a typical web page that featured a 20% Off coupon. The second version was a boiled-down page that showed the game with a Buy Now button.

Sales were 40% higher for the Buy Now option compared to the control version! Nobody would have expected that people would be more likely to buy if they didn't see a discount. EA discovered that by removing distractions, people were more likely to buy.[1]

Examples of targeted visual marketing campaigns

As companies learn to focus on select groups, visuals are a great way to engage a viewer with images that represent them. The challenge is how to spotlight one audience without alienating the others.

When Sephora launched its Color IQ system, it, along with partner Pantone, identified 10,000 different skin tones. Imagine identifying literally thousands of potential prospects who are looking to identify the products that work best with their skin tones. For many different reasons, it's obvious Sephora can't target 10,000 different audiences. But they were able to create groups of similar people.

When the beauty care company launched its first campaign based on the Color IQ system, it focused on Black business owners. The campaign spotlighted the influence of Black culture on beauty. Sephora created a short film and a series of print, digital, and video ads featuring Black women in different types of business settings.

One goal of the campaign was tied to Sephora's commitment to the Fifteen Percent Pledge, a call-to-action for retailers to dedicate 15% of their shelf space to Black-owned brands, since Black people make up 15% of the US population.[2]

This campaign also allowed Sephora's potential customers to see themselves in advertising and marketing campaigns. When people are able to see visuals with people who look like them interacting with your product, it's far easier for them to envision themselves buying and using your product.

Knowing your audience should define who you show in your visuals. Sometimes it's as simple as showing the right age or gender of your target audience. You wouldn't send an AARP catalog to someone in their late 20s.

Your target audience cannot be "everybody." If you don't create barriers for your marketing, your message will be too watered down to make an impact on anyone.

Talking to customers is the fastest way to figure out what they want. It's that simple. Ask the right questions, understand the data, do more of what works.

Don't just talk to the customers who decided to buy from you. It would be best to talk to prospects who didn't buy from you. Like the famous survivorship bias diagram, understanding where you failed will tell you more than studying your wins.

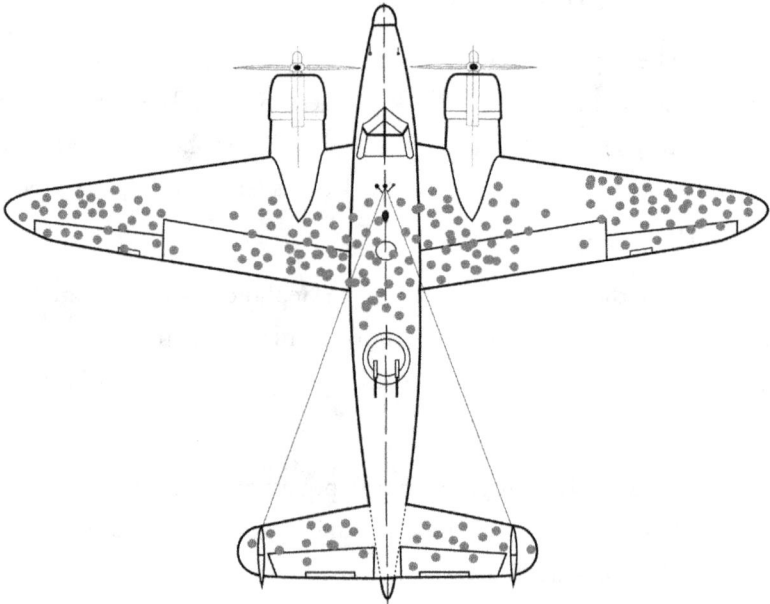

Figure 53: Survivorship bias

In case you don't know the story: In World War II, the American military studied the planes that returned from battle to see where they were being shot and where they should increase the metal plating. The problem is that these were the planes that survived the battle. The planes that didn't survive would show the most susceptible areas. Those are the areas that should have more armor.

Talking to prospects who didn't buy from you will show you where you need to strengthen your armor to be better prepared for the next (sales) battle.

Visual Cues

- Trust and a feeling of inclusion will strengthen customer and business bonds.

- Who you want to reach and who you can reach are often two different personas.

- Knowing who could be interested in your product or service, how they think, and how they act, can help shape the visual content you're creating.

- Understanding the demographics, psychographics, and behaviors of your target audience gives marketers an advantage to craft visuals that resonate on a deeper level, aligning with their audience's motivations.

- Your users will tell you what they want. You just have to listen.

- Don't just talk to the customers who decided to buy from you. Talk to those who didn't, also.

CHAPTER 6:

Competitive Insights

"Only a fool learns from his own mistakes. The wise man learns from the mistakes of others."

—*Otto von Bismarck*

Once you understand your customers and what they want, it's good to turn your attention to your competition. Talking to your customers will give you some insights about your competitors. It's human nature for them to make comparisons, and there is a high likelihood that your customers will evaluate your competition before deciding to buy from you.

Knowing your competition means you can identify the differences. This will help you amplify your strengths and minimize your weaknesses.

How to conduct a SWOT analysis of your and your competitors' visual marketing

Usually, running a SWOT analysis is the process of building out a 2x2 grid with boxes for Strengths, Weaknesses, Opportunities, and Threats, where you compare your business to another. An exercise like this allows you to define and identify areas for improvement and where your competition might be missing something important. There are many different areas of the business where you can run this exercise.

SWOT Assessment

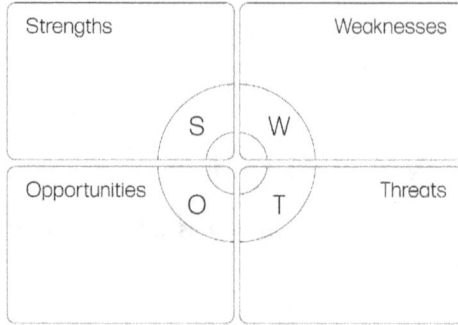

Figure 54: SWOT assessment

When it comes to creating a SWOT analysis for visual marketing, you'll have to evaluate your visual marketing efforts and compare them to your competitors'. This is where customer research can be helpful.

It's easy to become enamored with your own work, which can make it difficult to be objective in your evaluation. Discover what your potential audience thinks of your visuals. The feedback you gather during customer/prospect interviews can help inform this exercise.

I know you think your work is strong. Otherwise, you wouldn't have produced it. But it may not be the strength you think it is. This is where the effectiveness of the visuals should be evaluated. The assets that perform well should be classified as a strength. You can also include visuals that fill an empty space within the industry. Relying on data helps remove your subjectivity.

Weaknesses will reveal themselves with lower-performing visual marketing assets. Or if you have assets that look like those of your competitors, that could be seen as a weakness. You can't differentiate your visuals by fitting in. If the average prospect thinks your visual marketing assets belong to another company in your field, that's a weakness. It's potentially a liability if someone likes your work and mentally attributes it to a competitor.

Look for visual marketing areas where your competitors are not participating. For example, if nobody in your space creates short-form videos, that is a new chance to reach your target audience differently. Infographics were everywhere for a while in the early 2010s. What if now is the time to lean into this content type again? Where is there an industry-wide content gap that you could fill?

If you are having success with your visual marketing, you could see some of your competitors start to mimic what has been working well for you. If you're finding success with short-form video, don't be surprised if a competitor threatens your leadership position with this type of content. Or if you're using a particular kind of photo treatment or color scheme, your competitors might adopt similar visual marketing techniques.

Challengers always take on the incumbents; at one point or another, every company was a challenger. Early in my career, when I designed baseball caps for '47 Brand, I invented a way to use visor stitching as a design element, not just a functional element. At the time, '47 was much smaller than its competitors (namely New Era, Nike, and Reebok). Imagine my surprise when I saw my design on caps Reebok produced for the NBA Finals champions. Reebok saw '47 as a growing threat and "adopted" some of the visuals '47 had been developing. This example is product feature theft rather than visual marketing theft, but the concept is the same.

The popular communication platform Slack uses playful, bright visuals in its marketing. This is a strength in its competitive landscape that tends to lean more toward corporate design. However, reliance on hand-drawn illustrations could be a weakness when reaching more formal, conservative companies.

Identifying gaps and opportunities in the market

As mentioned in Chapter 5, the best way to identify gaps and opportunities in the market is to take inventory and talk to customers and prospects. When you are evaluating gaps, there are a few things you should be looking for:

- Image style (photos, illustrations)
- Colors (primary, secondary)
- Typography (what type of typeface are they using? Serif, sans-serif, bold, blocky, thin, script)
- Balance between type and imagery (what is more dominant, copy or imagery?)
- Types of visuals being created (static, animated, which type for each)
- Layout (does the visual move the viewer's eye around the canvas?)
- Design style (clean, grunge, art deco, nostalgic, etc.)

If you put these into a Miro or Pinterest board, you'll see trends start to develop. On the Pinterest board below, you'll notice that Intel uses similar visual themes in its advertising. Blue is a dominant factor in everything it does. The tech giant also relies on minimal, thin type in white or yellow. If your business competes against Intel, you could find a contrasting color and/or type style to help stand apart.

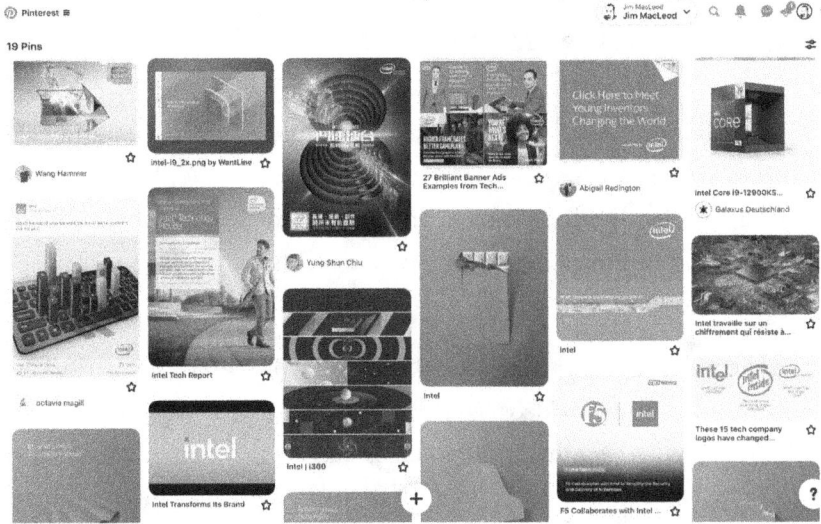

Figure 55: Pinterest board of Intel ads

Next, you'll want to look at adjacent industries to see what types of visuals they use. If you are responsible for marketing glucose testers, what types of visual marketing are companies using in dentistry or computer memory? Finding industries with some crossover use case or, even better, crossover customers can help you find some white space you can fill.

Usually, the same customer will buy different products in different categories. Make sure you're not inadvertently drifting into another category that may confuse the customer. If you're selling analytics software, that buyer may also buy account-based marketing software. You don't want the buyer to think they're looking at ABM collateral and dismiss you.

In this context, when I reference white space I mean an area that a competitor doesn't currently occupy. This is not to be confused with white space in your visuals, which is a very good thing. We'll dig into it more later, but white space in design is your friend.

Learning from the successes and failures of competitors' visual strategies

AI is making it hard to see your competitors' failed visual strategies. Thanks to systems such as Google Ads, the software instantly updates and optimizes the best-performing ads. You and I don't even have to do the evaluation and optimization work anymore. This means far fewer people see the under-performing ads.

On the video front, you can scroll through your competitors' YouTube channel(s) to see which videos have the most views. One thing that is hard to evaluate is whether any of those videos had a paid component. A video could be bad and still have hundreds of thousands of views if the company put ad dollars behind the effort to promote it.

More likely than not, a company isn't going to spend a lot of money promoting a bad video (though that's never stopped Hollywood). So, it's up to you to guess if a video's views result from an accompanying ad spend.

Social media is probably the most accessible place to evaluate whether a competitor's visual content performed well. One thing that's important to know is how those platforms work. Many platforms, like LinkedIn or X, deprioritize content that links to external sources. If a social media post has an amazing graphic but links to a blog post, the graphic can't be blamed for the post not performing.

When you understand how the platforms work, you can properly evaluate what visuals did or didn't perform well. Look at the posts that performed well to see what types of visuals they were using. This will help tell you what your audience is looking for … and what they're not.

Years ago, I used a platform called TrackMaven (now a part of Skyword) to evaluate how competitors were doing across social and public relations. One of our competitors had a video blowing everything out of water across the industry. When I clicked to learn more, it turned out it was a television commercial starring Peter Dinklage at the height of his Game of Thrones popularity. This is what happens when you're competing against a Fortune 100 company. While there was no way we'd be able to compete on that level, I learned we needed to invest more in video because our competition was going all-in on video at the time.

Benchmarking your visual content against industry standards

The ongoing evaluation of your visual content is critical to its success. If you don't have dashboard tools to automate metrics, setting up a spreadsheet is not too difficult. The hard part is carving out the time to take regular measurements.

If you have to measure your visual content manually, I recommend setting up a spreadsheet to track the following information:

Link to asset (so you can see what you're reporting on)

Date

Content

Content Type (image, text, combo)

Platform

Engagements (this can be broken down by comments, shares, likes, etc., but make sure you have a 'total' column)

Asset Name	Content Type	Date	Link	Platform	Shares	Likes	Comments	Impressions	Downloads	Total Engagements
Effective Classroom Managen	Blog post	11/20/25	https://ebn.	Blog	1	0	0	153		154
Daily School Leadership Insig	Social	11/21/25	https://ebn.	LinkedIn	1	82	17	90		190
Daily School Leadership Insig	Social	11/21/25	https://ebn.	Instagram	0	12	3	22		37
Creating a Positive Learning E	Social	11/22/25	https://ebn.	Facebook	0	132	19	554		705
Creating a Positive Learning E	Social	11/22/25	https://ebn.	Instagram	0	5	1	19		26
Choosing the Right Curriculur	Blog post	11/23/25	https://ebn.	Blog	0	0	0	227		227
Creative School Decoration Id	Social	11/24/25	https://ebn.	Instagram	9	32	21	67		129
School Q&A Session	Podcast	11/27/25	https://ebn.	Apple					17	17
School Q&A Session	Podcast	11/27/25	https://ebn.	Spotify					3	3
School Q&A Session	Podcast	11/27/25	https://ebn.	Google					9	9
Top 5 Tools for New Teachers	Social	11/28/25	https://ebn.	Facebook	12	53	7	482		554
What to do When a Sentinel A	Blog post	11/29/25	https://ebn.	Blog	0	0	0	1810		1810
Education Trends 2025	Video	11/30/25	https://ebn.	YouTube	0	22	6	279		307
Sustainable School Practices	Social	12/1/25	https://ebn.	LinkedIn	3	15	3	118		139
Sustainable School Practices	Social	12/1/25	https://ebn.	Instagram	0	3	0	52		55
Academic Year Planning Guide	eBook	12/4/25	https://ebn.	Resource C	0	0	0	190		190
Academic Year Planning Guide	Social	12/5/25	https://ebn.	Facebook	12	626	210	1123		1971

Figure 56: Content measurement

Find a time to measure your visual content on a regular basis. When you're first creating your content strategy, you'll want to set the cadence for when you'll be reviewing the data you're collecting.

While it's essential to have a statistically viable data set, early on you'll want to evaluate this in shorter intervals. Checking the data more frequently helps you make changes without spending time and money unnecessarily on poor-performing content. If you go too long before evaluating, you could be serving visual content that doesn't work for longer than you have to.

The most important thing is finding time to repeat the measurement. Depending on the platform, you may not be able to collect this data later.

Once your content gets more solidified, I'd recommend collecting the data monthly. The first of the month is a good time to look into this. I like to set a monthly calendar placeholder to collect and evaluate data. This isn't fun for most people, so build in as many excuse-preventors as possible.

As you collect the data, you'll be able to sort it based on whatever metric you've deemed most important. You may want to have a few KPIs that you track to help evaluate effectiveness through different lenses.

If it's working, keep doing that!

Tools for competitive analysis and monitoring

If you're doing competitive analysis and monitoring for the first time, I suggest finding a do-it-yourself way to trial this activity. Buying a tool without determining how you'll manage this is probably going to be a bad use of your money.

As I mentioned in Chapter 5, you can set up a Pinterest board (or boards) with your competitor's visual marketing efforts. Once you've set this up and established the habit of pinning visuals you see, you can set up a spreadsheet to track engagement metrics.

All you have to do is create the same spreadsheet you created to monitor your content, but change the link to point to pins on your competitive Pinterest board. Again, you'll want to be able to see the content you're evaluating quickly. Then, follow your regular cadence to collect and put the data into the spreadsheet.

With the rapid evolution of ChatGPT and future AI agent tools, there is likely a way to automate this work. Since it's such an emerging space, whatever I recommend today could be replaced by a better tool by the time you read this.

In the meantime, there are always paid solutions like Hootsuite, Semrush, SimilarWeb, or Sprout Social that can monitor competitive activities. Some tools, like Semrush or SimilarWeb, can provide deeper analytics into your competitors' activities. This allows you to monitor their most shared content and adjust your visual strategy accordingly.

Strategies for differentiating your brand's visual content

Once you understand what your competitors are doing, finding the visual areas they are missing is much easier. While it's vital to zig when they're zagging, be sure you don't go too far away from what your customers and prospects might expect. There needs to be some familiarity mixed in somewhere.

If Goldman Sachs suddenly started releasing marketing that looked like a Swedish death metal band, people would look right past it because they wouldn't think it's marketing provided by one of the world's leading financial institutions.

Figure 57: Death metal version of Goldman Sachs logo

You don't want this effect.

It's one thing to stand out from the crowd. It's another to stand in the wrong crowd.

The US has two major private courier companies: UPS and FedEx. But did you know DHL has roughly the same global revenue? In 2002, DHL updated its logo to add yellow because, according to the logo developers, it was a "fast" color. It's also been rumored (meaning it's on Wikipedia but not linked to a specific source) that the yellow comes from a partnership DHL[1] had with a Formula One team that used yellow as its primary color.

DHL's use of yellow and red has helped differentiate it from UPS's brown and FedEx's white with purple and orange. When you see a DHL truck on the highway, there's no mistaking it. UPS trademarked its brown color within its industry because it is so synonymous with the earth tone. FedEx (with the hidden arrow in the logo) and DHL's bright yellow and red help let the viewer know their service is fast.

Figure 58: Unsplash: UPS: Rosa Rafael, DHL: Maxim, FedEx: Toni Pomar

Find the visual space where your competitors aren't participating and start trying things. Run campaigns and, if possible, run A/B tests to see which visuals resonate best with prospects. You should always be testing and discovering better ways to communicate visually.

As much as you are watching your competitors, they're also likely to monitor the work you produce. If you do something that works better than expected, it shouldn't surprise you if your competitors do something similar. Industries going after the same customers will do things proven to work. It's easier to iterate than create.

The good news is that if you're the one who came up with something creative that others imitated, you have the ability to create something else even more exciting.

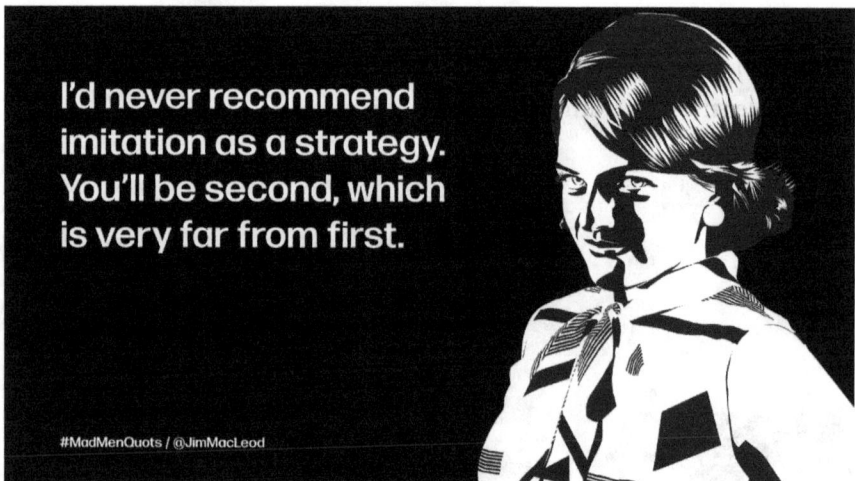

Figure 59: Mad Men illustration by Jim MacLeod

Visual Cues

- When you are evaluating gaps, there are a few things you should be looking for:

  - Image style (photos, illustrations)
  - Colors (primary, secondary)
  - Typography (what type of typeface are they using? Serif, sans-serif, bold, blocky, thin, script)

- Balance between type and imagery (what is more dominant, copy or imagery?)
- Types of visuals being created (static, animated, which type for each)
- Layout (does the visual move the viewer's eye around the canvas?)
- Design style (clean, grunge, art deco, nostalgic, etc.)

- AI is so good at optimizing ads, it's hard to see weaknesses in competitors' work.
- Make time to measure your content on a regular basis.
- Stand out from your competition, but not too far. You don't want to create confusion.

CHAPTER 7:

Content Relevance and Selection

"Content builds relationships. Relationships are built on trust. Trust drives revenue."

—*Andrew Davis*

You've done your audience research. You've done your industry research. Now it's time to determine what visual marketing content you will produce.

This job would be much easier if all content resonated with every audience. Unfortunately, it doesn't. Each audience has its preferences, and the effectiveness of the content differs for each audience. A TikTok campaign might not work great if you sell products to senior citizens. If you're trying to hype up a sneaker drop, you probably don't want to run an ad on TV during the five o'clock local news (though that would be a unique way to announce it).

Running marketing campaigns with content your audience will ignore wastes time, energy, and money. These two scenarios wouldn't work because those particular audiences aren't on those platforms. They're never going to see your visual marketing efforts.

It's a chicken-and-egg scenario where you can either determine what content your audience consumes or start with the platforms and work backward to the content type. Often the content and platform preferences will feed into each other because only certain types of content can be displayed on certain platforms. You can't post a white paper to YouTube (but, in Chapter 13, we'll talk about how to get content from white papers onto a platform like YouTube).

The goal is to create content that builds trust and inspires prospects to buy from you. To do that, you must create the content your audience wants to consume.

Criteria for determining the relevance of visual content

Your audience has preferences regarding the types of content they consume. It's not about the content *you* want to create; it's about what *they* want to consume. You can be the best Flash animator in the world, but if nobody is consuming Flash content anymore (thanks, Apple), you're wasting your time creating Flash-based content.

Understanding your audience's wants and needs empowers you to produce content they want to consume. For prospects higher up the corporate food chain, the content needs to be easy to consume and data-based. They don't have time to get into the details. They're concerned about two things: Will it work, and will I get fired if I buy this?

Data helps in these situations, but this audience isn't necessarily looking for infographics because they're savvy enough to know that good design can obfuscate numbers that don't make business sense. Some C-level executives are skeptical when they see great visuals because design can be used like a magic trick. The viewer can get distracted by something eye-catching and end up missing valuable information.

This type of audience is looking for straightforward, informative content. You have to use clean visuals that convey high-level information and provide an easy pathway to additional context if they're looking for it.

This is just one type of audience. Different audiences want to consume different types of content, so it's up to you to produce the right content for the right audience.

Matching visual content types with marketing objectives and audience preferences

At the different stages of the buyer's journey, different content types should be used. The buyer's journey typically consists of three stages in a funnel—going from Awareness (what is my problem?) to Consideration (can this product solve my problem?) to Decision (is this the right product and business to solve my problem?). It's a funnel because buyers focus on fewer and fewer companies as they go through their exploration. The list of people who fit into each stage gets smaller as you get closer to the sales stage.

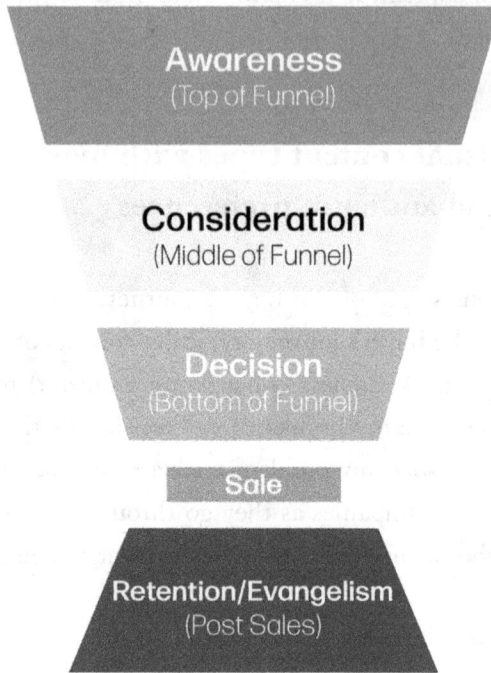

Figure 60: Sales/Marketing funnel

This diagram also includes post-sales content. Keeping your customers engaged is more important than finding new customers. A first-time customer can cost between 5-25 times as much as retaining an existing customer.[1] Hunting (new customers) can be fun and exciting, but farming (retaining current customers) is easier and cheaper for the company.

Besides, you don't want to end up like the man-looking-at-a-new-girl meme. If you're only focused on new customers, your existing customers will feel like the annoyed woman on the right.

Figure 61: iStock.com/Antonio Guillem

There are many variations of this diagram regarding the content associated with each stage of the funnel, but I've found that this content/funnel map works pretty well for B2B audiences:

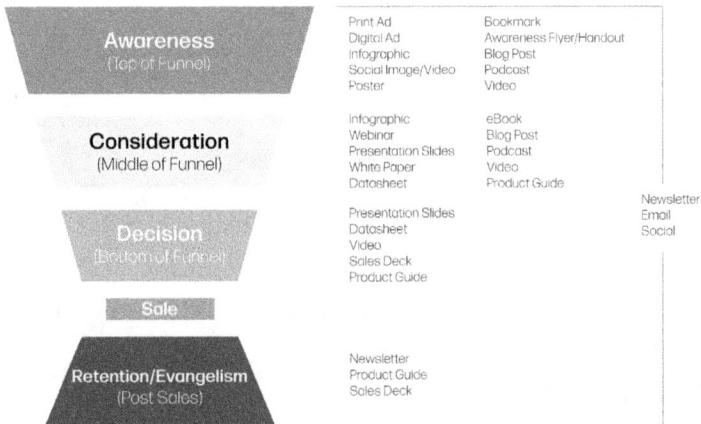

Awareness (Top of Funnel)	Print Ad Digital Ad Infographic Social Image/Video Poster	Bookmark Awareness Flyer/Handout Blog Post Podcast Video	
Consideration (Middle of Funnel)	Infographic Webinar Presentation Slides White Paper Datasheet	eBook Blog Post Podcast Video Product Guide	
Decision (Bottom of Funnel)	Presentation Slides Datasheet Video Sales Deck Product Guide		Newsletter Email Social
Sale			
Retention/Evangelism (Post Sales)	Newsletter Product Guide Sales Deck		

Figure 62: Sales/marketing funnel with content for each stage

Some content (such as emails, newsletters, and social visuals) goes across the entire buyer's journey. This diagram lists a wide array of visual content types. You'll probably have others that aren't on here, and you'll probably see some on this list that don't make sense for your business.

This is a general guide. There are some content types, like webinars, that can be used across the entire lifecycle. Even though webinars are listed in the Consideration and Decision phases, they could also be used to help identify the problem (Awareness) and keep existing customers engaged by promoting new features (Retention/Evangelism). As we discussed, it's vital to keep existing customers engaged. Having current customers speak as featured guests on a webinar addresses two problems at once: it keeps the current customer engaged, and it's social proof that a customer can buy your product and find success. We'll get deeper into this in Chapter.[11]

The role of context in content selection and creation

The foundation under every piece of content you create should align with the problems the viewer is trying to solve. When you keep this context in mind, it helps shape everything you do.

Some audiences love short-form videos. For these people, YouTube Shorts or Instagram Reels (or any of the myriad copycats) could be the perfect platform to reach the right audiences.

TikTok might seem like an app for mindless scrolling, but valuable brand content is being shared on there. According to HubSpot,[2] there are three main areas where marketers can succeed on short-form video:

Influencer Marketing

They understand the platform and can create engaging videos for your audience

Original Content

Quickly hopping on a trend can help get recognition

Paid ads

Running ads can help level the field when competing with big players

Marketers spent $3.8 billion on TikTok in 2023. According to analysis by Insider Intelligence and eMarketer, TikTok is on pace to surpass Facebook in total daily minutes in 2025.[3] This is a huge turnaround for an app that was known as Musical.ly and let teens and preteens create lip-sync videos.

Much like blogging in the 2000s, short-form videos started off as a teen phenomenon and evolved into a mainstream platform. And, also like blogging, companies who jumped in early have seen success.

Brands that create exciting visual content will perform best on platforms like TikTok. WWE has millions of followers, and its content is tailor-made for a platform like TikTok. Editing exciting match footage combined with music and overly enthusiastic commentary lets viewers get a taste of what they're missing by not watching the full broadcasts.

WWE also uses TikTok to show behind-the-scenes content or interactions with fans that normally wouldn't make it into a broadcast. This audience understands what they see on the surface and what happens behind the curtain are two different things. For a rabid fanbase, getting more content that, while curated, doesn't feel overproduced is extremely valuable. It helps strengthen the bonds the audience feels towards the wrestlers and the overall WWE brand.

The 2023 romantic comedy, "Anyone But You," originally earned a scant $8 million during its debut weekend. The distributor, Sony, then began urging TikTok users to recreate a sequence from the movie. Positive word of mouth helped, but the movie turned into a $219 million hit with the help of TikTok tapping into the target audience for the movie.

Hollywood now leans on short-form video to launch movies. It has seen similar success with films such as M3gan, Wonka, and Barbie. 25.2% of TikTok's U.S. users are in the coveted 18-24 age group.[4] Overall, half of the population in the U.S., around 170 million people, use TikTok.[5] Companies would be shooting themselves in the foot if they were not using TikTok to go after certain core audiences.

| #Barbenheimer | #DeadpoolAndWolverine | #AnyoneButYou |

Figure 63: TikToks for movie promotion

If you have young people in your orbit, pay attention to the content they're consuming and the platforms they're using. It probably means you'll have to create some sort of campaign for that platform in the next few years. They're always on the bleeding edge because they don't want to be where their parents/grandparents are spending time. Young people started on Facebook, and then the adults moved in. So the kids moved to Instagram. Then the parents moved there, so the kids moved to TikTok. The next generation will probably move somewhere else.

This is one reason why some new platforms are difficult to use. Complicated user interfaces can be seen as a benefit if they keep "the olds" like me out.

Peloton is a well-known brand that uses different platforms to share different types of visual content. For example, on Instagram, Peloton highlights community-building visuals and sharing user stories. Over on YouTube, it focuses on instructional videos and product demonstrations. This ensures its visuals align with each platform's strengths.

Techniques for ensuring content diversity and freshness

When was the last time you did a content audit? I'm going to go out on a limb and say the answer is probably, "Not recently." If you don't have a tool that reports on your content, broken down by type, audience, vertical, etc., then you should make a spreadsheet that allows you to get an overview of what you have.

Create a spreadsheet with the following fields:

- Title
- Date Published
- Subject/Topic
- Product/Product line (these might need to be separated)
- Persona
- Vertical
- Buying Stage
- Performance (based on date)
- Changes in Performance (based on date)
- Notes

You can then filter by different aspects to help identify content gaps. Do you have 27 case studies for your healthcare vertical but no webinars for the Consideration phase? Now you know what to create next … as long as those assets will perform well for the given audience. Every audience in each demographic will respond differently to varying points of the customer lifecycle, so make sure you're recording the performance of the assets to determine what you should do next.

You should have multiple Performance columns, one for each date you're measuring the asset. After each of these should be a Changes in Performance column. This way you can see changes after each interval. I also like to put in conditional logic so if the percent change is positive, the number turns green. If it's negative, the number turns red.

If you're lacking time to create fresh content (and I know you are, because everyone is), you can find ways to refresh and/or repurpose content. We'll get further into this in Chapter 9, but know that content is ready for a refresh when it stops performing as well as it should.

Tools for content planning and scheduling

There are so many content operations systems at the enterprise level. I've had success using an array of products from Workfront to Kapost, Monday. com to Smartsheet. Many of these SaaS tools allow you to build out processes for creating content. Some can also help with sharing and tracking revisions throughout the process.

If you're looking to build a content plan, there are many tool options in this space. Personally, I use Notion to plan and track my projects. Other systems like Airtable, Trello, or Basecamp can help you plan your content operations.

Automating the scheduling publication of content can be harder because sometimes you need integrations to publish to different platforms. Some of the aforementioned tools can give you a calendar view of all in-progress and completed projects so you can see when they were finished, distributed, or deployed. This can be incredibly helpful if you run many email campaigns. You want to make sure you're not spamming your target audience with multiple messages in a short amount of time. That's one of the fastest ways to turn a subscriber into an unsubscriber.

Publish Date	Due Date	Owner	Status	Title/Topic	Type	Notes
11/20/25	11/15/25	Nate Summers	In Progress	Effective Classroom Management Tips	Blog post	Review latest gardenting trends for inclusion
11/21/25	11/16/25	Anna Marie	Waiting	Daily School Leadership Insights	Social post	Confirm image selections
11/22/25	11/17/25	James Howlett	Waiting	Creating a Positive Learning Environment	Social post	Source images from recent indoor collection
11/23/25	11/20/25	Kurt Wagner	Pending Approval	Choosing the Right Curriculum	Blog post	Send to John for final proofreading
11/24/25	11/21/25	Anna Marie	Done	Creative School Decoration Ideas	Social post	Posted successfully
11/27/25	11/22/25	Nate Summers	Done	School Q&A Session	Podcast	Episode released
11/28/25	11/23/25	James Howlett	Waiting	Top 5 Tools for New Teachers	Social post	Finalize graphics
11/29/25	11/24/25	James Howlett	In Progress	What to do when a Sentinel attacks	Blog post	Include tips
11/30/25	11/24/25	Kurt Wagner	Stuck	Education Trends 2025	Video	Waiting for budget approval
12/1/25	11/28/25	Anna Marie	Done	Sustainable School Practices	Social post	schedule for morning post
12/4/25	11/29/25	Rob Drake	Waiting	Academic Year Planning Guide	eBook	Wlating on final illustrations
12/5/25	12/1/25	James Howlett	In Progress	Academic Year Planning Guide	Social post	Gather content from last week's posts

Figure 64: Content calendar

Creative teams are often at the center of most content creation. They will have better visibility into all the ongoing projects than anyone else in your marketing team. If you have a project-minded creative director, she or he will be able to be the wide-angle lens across the department.

Tools are useful, but it's invaluable to have that one person on the team who will speak up in a meeting to say, "May 15th isn't the best day to launch [campaign A] because [campaign B] is also scheduled for that day." This helps protect the prospects who will be exposed to both campaigns and the internal team members who worked hard on these different campaigns. Nobody wants their work to be diluted or ignored because of poor planning.

Measuring and analyzing content performance for continuous improvement

You probably noticed one of the fields I suggested for your content spreadsheet was "Performance." There's a reason why John Doer wrote *Measure What Matters*. You need to know how things are performing to determine what to do next.

It's important to be data-informed rather than data-driven. There's a difference between data *suggesting* what to do next and data *telling* you what to do next. Especially in the realm of visuals, data can help confirm the work you should be doing. The data will show you trends on how assets are performing. The notes section in your tracking tool will also give additional context as to why an asset was performing well or not.

If an asset underperformed, it's time to make something new.

If engagement is slowly winding down, it's probably time for a refresh. What can you do to update this asset? This is the question you should ask for any asset before starting something new. It's much easier to update an asset than to create something from scratch.

If an asset did well and then engagement fell off a cliff, there is probably an outside reason for that. Was there a change to your website? Did Apple change the iPhone Mail settings again? Were you shadow-banned on social media? Is there a problem with your email provider and are your emails getting flagged as spam? Looking at the data of your visual content could help identify much larger problems. That bright yellow eBook could be the figurative canary in the coal mine.

I know you picked up this book to learn about visual marketing and all I've done is tell you to make spreadsheets. But this work is important and informs the rest of the book. This work may not be as fun as creating visual content, but it will save you time. Seeing your content's performance will help ensure that you're producing the right visual content.

Otherwise, you're just creating content and checking the "done" box. Nobody wants to waste their time, money, or energy creating useless content, and your business doesn't need it. Doing this up-front work will ensure that the visual content you're creating will help solve a problem for your business.

The next step is working to create content that is on brand and helps tell a consistent story.

Visual Cues

- It's a chicken-and-egg scenario where you can either determine what content your audience consumes or start with the platforms and work backward to the content type.
- It's not about the content you want to create; it's about what they want to consume.
- The people buying your product are concerned about two things: Will it work, and will I get fired if I buy this? Your content has to address these concerns.
- Different content works best for different phases of the sales/marketing funnel.
- Your visual marketing content should align with the problems the buyer is trying to solve.
- Use tools or spreadsheets to track your content creation, calendar, and analytics.

CHAPTER 8

Brand Identity and Visual Guidelines

"The brand style guide is your shield against bad ideas."

—Jim MacLeod

Your visual brand identity is one of your business's most valuable marketing assets. It tells the world who you are. There's a reason people have an emotional response when they see some companies' logos: They have feelings tied to that logo, and each time they see it, those feelings are reinforced.

Brands show their logos repeatedly and consistently to make them familiar. The smile/arrow in the Amazon logo, connecting the A to the Z, can now be used without the Amazon wordmark because people have been exposed to it many times. From the app on your phone to the packages in your driveway to the shipping trucks on the highway, the Amazon smile has become so ubiquitous that you don't have to read the word to know it represents one of the world's largest companies.

Figure 65: Unsplash.com | Wicked Monday

The fact that a yellow/orange (or black, in this case) curved arrow equals a company that delivers whatever you need is not an accident. This can only happen because there is strong visual brand adherence to the style guide. You don't see the smile/arrow out of certain contexts, in different colors, or mixed with other logos. Amazon's strict guidelines around its logo and its usage have trained people on what that curved arrow means.

Whether you think positively or negatively when you see this logomark depends on your interactions with the overall Amazon brand. For now, we'll stay focused on the brand's visual aspects.

While this example is focused on one of the largest companies in the world, it also applies to the smallest of businesses. Establishing good visual habits when a company is small will pay off when the company gets bigger. Nike paid $35 for its logo design. Nobody knew the global behemoth it would become one day. Small and medium businesses must take visual marketing as seriously as the giants.

Brand, identity, and visual guidelines: Why the fuss?

Did you see the new blue bottles of Coca-Cola?

How about when Google changed its home screen to black and red with purple text links?

Do you remember the time Facebook replaced the "f" icon with an actual face?

Of course not. None of these things would happen since these companies have strict brand guidelines. Because they have strong brand guidelines, you already know what the Coca-Cola red, the Google home page, and the Facebook "f" icon look like.

The fact that you can picture all three of these in your mind is why these businesses stick with these existing visuals. Money alone can't buy brand recognition like these companies have. It takes time, repetition, and money to establish brand recognition on this level.

Coca-Cola was the 15th most valuable brand in the Kantar BrandZ 2024 ranking.[1]

It is estimated that Coca-Cola's brand value is over $106 billion.[2] So, apparently, there is a dollar amount you could spend to build that brand recognition. I'm going to guess you don't have that in this year's marketing budget.

Questions to ask when establishing a comprehensive visual brand style guide

When a visual brand is first being created, certain decisions must be made. Will you use photographs? Will those be professional or candids? Will they have an effect used to create consistency?

If you're not using photos, are you using illustrations? Iconography? What color will you be known for? How about typography? Bold type? Handwritten? Serif (letters with little hats and feet) or sans-serif (letters without the flourishes at the ends) fonts?

These are all questions that need to be answered when establishing the visual brand. While this can be a lot of fun, it is very difficult to do correctly.

We've already discussed that you should know what your competitors are doing in your space with their visuals. Once you've identified the areas where you can visually stand out from your competition, you can start to put together the pieces of your new brand identity.

Key components of visual brand identity (logo, color palette, typography, and more)

Remember, a brand is so much more than a logo. A brand is every inter-action your customers and prospects have with your products, services, and company. While a logo is part of a visual brand identity, do not confuse it with a brand.

Your logo should be clear and memorable. By clear, I mean legible. People should be able to read your logo. It should have your company name and, if possible, something that visually lets the viewer know what your company offers.

For many years Dunkin's logo had a coffee cup because the company wanted people to know that Dunkin' is a great source to get their daily coffee fix. Part of the problem was the original name, Dunkin' Donuts. Originally, it was a doughnut shop located in the northeast of the United States. As buying trends evolved, Dunkin' Donuts had to change people's perception of the company. In this case, Dunkin' Donuts needed to pivot from doughnuts to coffee. It took many years, but eventually the company was able to drop the "Donuts" part of its name.

Figure 66: Dunkin' Donuts logo history

Having firmly established itself as a coffee shop, the new Dunkin' logo was able to drop the coffee cup from its primary logo, but you'll still see it on products and in-store. This has been an ongoing visual brand evolution for a massive company, so it takes time to complete a transition this significant.

The right logo mark will allow you to explore consistent visual elements. The IT networking giant Cisco has a stylized version of the Golden Gate Bridge, tying back its San Francisco heritage. The rounded pill-shapes have been used across Cisco's visual marketing for years.

Figure 67: Cisco Systems logo

One of the first things people may recognize about your company will be the color. Many companies work to "own" their brand color. As we discussed in Chapter 1, Owens-Corning owns the trademark to its pink insulation. Coca-Cola calls its red its "second secret formula."[3] For more than 130 years, when you see that red, you know what you're going to get.

Other companies that have invested a lot into owning their color:

- The Home Depot (orange)
- T-Mobile (magenta)
- Tiffany & Co. (egg blue)
- Post Its (yellow)
- UPS (brown)
- John Deere (green and yellow)

Most of these businesses have gone as far as trademarking their color to protect it from competitors trying to cash in on the brand equity these industry leaders have built up over time.

A 2017 study revealed that 69-90% of a consumer's initial judgment is based on color.[4] People ascribe brand values based on the company logo and colors during their first impression. The color you choose and how you present it matter a lot in people's initial impressions of your brand.

Typography also adds to or detracts from brand perception. Companies that use serif typefaces can be seen as more regal and upscale. Serifs help increase legibility and are perceived as more elegant, classic, and a mark of establishment. On the flip side, san-serif typefaces are better for online experiences due to screen resolutions.

I'm sure you've heard of typeface Times New Roman. It was initially designed for the British newspaper *The Times* because serif typefaces are easier to read in large chunks of copy. The serifs help keep your eye focused on that line of copy. After, it was adopted by the New York Times and many, many other print-based companies. Because of the consistent use of serif typefaces in formal applications, people have a built-in predisposition to think of these companies as more prestigious.

Let's take a minute to define fonts and typefaces. Back in the days of setting type by hand, a typeface was sold with multiple fonts. The typeface is the name and style of the type. Examples: Times, Helvetica, Arial, Comic Sans (ugh). The font is the size and style.

Typeface: Helvetica

- Font: Helvetica 14pt, italic
- Font: Helvetica 24pt, black

Typeface: Times

- Font: Times 24pt, regular
- Font: Times 12pt, bold

Typeface: Arial

- Font: Arial 9pt, bold
- Font: Arial 10pt, italic

Fun fact: when these metal letters were sold and stored in a box, the capital letters were stored in the upper part of the case (uppercase), and the non-capital letters were stored in the lower part of the case (lowercase).

Figure 68: iStock.com/zlikovec

Trust me, if you use the term "typeface" correctly with a designer, they'll be impressed and know you're smarter than the average bear regarding typography and design. Microsoft used the term "font" in Word when they should have used "typeface," and the words have been corrupted ever since.

What elements will you use with your visual marketing? It's good to have some consistent element in your visual marketing. Will it be something like Cisco where you use the pill-shaped element from the logo? Or a unique bright green border like Hulu uses in its visual marketing? Whatever you choose, it should be used across all your visual marketing. This repetition creates a mental shortcut for the people viewing your marketing. They'll learn that when they see something like earth tones, hand-written type and simple stick figure illustrations, they are probably looking at Life Is Good's marketing materials.

Once you've established the logo, colors, type treatment, and elements, you're ready to start building out your visual marketing.

Implementing brand identity consistently across all visual content

Using your visual marketing elements consistently leads people to recognize it as your marketing and instantly ascribe the affinity they have for your brand to that marketing message.

Think of it as a shortcut to brand recognition.

You don't have to smell or taste french fries, but as soon as you see McDonald's golden arches, you know what to expect. McDonald's has done an amazing amount of marketing with the yellow M on a red background. They've even managed to brand their visual brand. When I say "golden arches," you automatically know what that means. When I described it as a yellow M on a red background, that sounds lifeless or clinical. There is a playfulness in McDonald's marketing that isn't obvious when described this way. Luckily, most of us can picture what I mean by saying, "yellow M on a red background."

It's possible you even heard ba-da-ba-BA-BAAA in your head because McDonald's has done such a great job tying that little jingle[5] to their brand. As Mickey-D's expands further globally, we're seeing less and less of the McDonald's wordmark. The golden arches on red are enough to let the viewer know what they're seeing.

Repetition and consistency are the most important part of establishing a visual brand.

These companies have very strict rules around the use of their logos, colors, and typography. The 2024 Olympic Brand Guidelines document is 137 pages long.[6] General Electric's 2008 identity program was 772 pages![7] (I bet some agency executives got nice bonuses after that deliverable.)

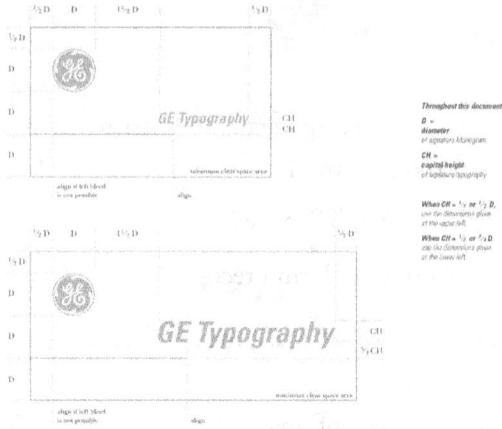

Figure 69: Page from GE's style guide

All joking aside, this type of documentation helps maintain brand consistency across multiple use cases. Think about how many vendors GE uses to produce its signage and marketing materials. Everything those myriad vendors produce must be on brand.

In 2023 GE split into three different companies, so there are even more potential points of visual brand failure. The GE logo now needs to be consistent across three companies as they work to capitalize on decades of GE brand equity. Each company has its own typeface and color, but the GE logo–the script initials dating back to the company's founding in the 1890s–is consistent.[8]

The role of brand guidelines in maintaining visual coherence

Brand guidelines help keep everyone on the same page when it comes to the visual brand. New employees, external vendors, and partners can be sure they understand what is expected from a visual brand standpoint.

Knowing the clearance space around a logo, the HEX and Pantone colors for the primary color, or what type of photography should be used, are all simple policies that can be followed to ensure visual coherence. If everyone follows these guidelines, it creates consistency. The thing to remember is the most successful visual marketing companies are always consistent.

I started this chapter with my quote, "The brand style guide is your shield against bad ideas," because we have all been put into the position where an executive gives us direction that may not fit into the actual brand. This is when you can point to the style guide, shrug, and say, "There's nothing we can do. It's against brand standards." This way, you're not the person telling a high-powered executive, "No,"—you're saying it's not possible because of pre-established guidelines. Hopefully you don't then have to explain the value of the brand to this executive.

The reality is you can probably change the brand style guide or bend the rules for that executive, but then you're not doing your job. If your job is to build the brand to help the company, you sometimes must be the bad cop, even if the person making the request is far above you on the org chart. If they do ask, you can now explain why it's essential for the business's success to be consistent with your visual branding.

Case studies of strong visual brand identities

I mentioned Tiffany & Co. earlier because that is a company that "owns" its color. You know what those famous little robin's-egg blue boxes look like without seeing them. Tiffany blue, as it is commonly called, was registered as a trademark in 1998 after the Supreme Court ruled on a different case. Supreme Court Justice Stephen Breyer wrote: "Color alone, at least sometimes, can meet the basic legal requirements for use as a trademark. It can act as a symbol that distinguishes a firm's goods and identifies their source, without serving any other significant function."[9]

So, you can own a color! Although the laws differ from country to country, know that you can own a color within certain use cases. For example, Tiffany & Co. has the color trademarked only in its boxes and bags.[10] Tiffany & Co. worked with Pantone to create a color only they can use. 1837 Blue (named after the year the company was founded) is the official name of the Pantone color.

The color represents femininity. It is soft and delicate while also strong, just like the robin's eggs it is reminiscent of. The color is so well known that if you saw a taxicab in 1837 blue, you'd wonder if it was tied to a promotion with Tiffany & Co.

And what does that mean for the brand? AdWeek declared it as "very possibly the most recognizable and most desired retail container in history." Tiffany & Co's consistent use of 1837 Blue has created a shortcut in people's minds that the contents of the box, even without being seen, are high quality, exclusive, and elegant. That is a brand that is worth billions.

Adobe is another company that strongly adheres to its brand style guide. For a company that offers dozens of products, each product line has a unique visual identity that still stays within Adobe's bounds.

Adobe has products that sell to consumers (B2C) as well as to businesses (B2B). This can be very challenging from a branding perspective, but Adobe is a master at balancing both audiences.

Adobe first gained prominence with its early design software. One of its brands, Photoshop, is practically a generic verb at this point (a big no-no in the world of branding). For a company rooted in design software, it makes sense that the tech giant is strict with its visual brand standards.

Adobe has used a stylized A since the company's beginning in 1982, originally designed by the founder's wife, Marva Warnock.[11] In 1993, the company introduced the knocked-out stylized A on a red color block ("knocked out" means there is no color in that space).

In 2023, Adobe's marketing started doing something uncommon for big brands: It rolled out a new Adobe mark that combines the stylized A as part of the wordmark, this time with thicker type. The problem is that this isn't the actual Adobe logo; it's just being used in marketing efforts.

If you're reading this and thinking, "What are they doing!?!" you're not alone. As I discussed over the past few pages, consistency is key. So why did Adobe roll out a logo that isn't actually a logo? Adobe's head of brand strategy and customer insights, Heather Combs, told Fast Company that the new treatment of the Adobe logo was to garner buzz and grab some attention as it introduces generative AI capabilities across its design software portfolio.[11]

Figure 70: Adobe corporate logo, and marketing logo

Combs told Fast Company, "Our objective is to put the Adobe brand in people's mouths to make them think about us and want to talk about us," she says. "If this new wordmark creates a point of interest, then it's doing its job." Adobe has started using the new marketing logo in its product logos. We're watching Adobe's visual identity evolution in real time.

The moral of the story is that if you have Adobe's brand value, feel free to roll out different logos in your marketing. I wouldn't suggest it, but it seems to be working for Adobe, so it's hard to say it's "wrong."

(But it is wrong.)

If you're curious why turning your brand into a verb is a branding mistake, it's due to a legal issue known as genericide. This is when an owned brand becomes so common that people start to use it as a verb. When a brand name becomes generic, it can be difficult to legally protect the brand.

Just like with Photoshop, this happens more often than you think. We often Google things. Or you might know someone who loves Rollerblading. We use Kleenex to wipe our noses. We used to Xerox pages. This can be great for brand recognition at first, but can cause legal and brand problems down the road.

Does anybody else remember "Zoom fatigue" from the early 2020s? During the time of the COVID-19 pandemic, Zoom became a verb for many people. When people grew weary of being on video calls all the time, Zoom was the recipient of the brand backlash. Verbifying brand names comes with potential downsides.[12]

Tools and software for brand guideline creation and dissemination

You now know why it's crucial to have brand guidelines and you've created your brand assets. The next step is to put that together in a package so others can easily consume and understand your guidelines.

Brandfolder

Brandfolder is a SaaS product from SmartSheet that allows you to easily build an online brand style guide. Creating a single source of truth for visual and written brand guidelines helps make it clear to everyone who uses these marketing assets.

Digital Brand Toolkit

What if you could fill out a questionnaire, pay a price, and get an entire brand kit delivered to you? That's what Digital Brand Toolkit does. This simple system gets to know the goals and vibe you want to hit and provides you with everything you need—from a logo to slide templates to YouTube cover images.

> *"Brand guidelines allow you to ramp up content production without losing your mind. It's your single source of truth that you can give to any vendor or employee who's representing your brand—online or off."*
>
> *—Hannah Szabo, Head of Operations, Digital Brand Kit*

Lytho

Lyto is a SaaS offering built for marketing and creative teams that have too much to do (that's all of us, right?). This system allows users to access assets, projects, feedback, and more, all in one place. It also allows people outside of the creative team to create on-brand content. Having a content repository built with content operations workflows can make life a lot easier for busy teams.

Distribution

When it comes to asset collection and distribution, you've probably worked somewhere that had a giant folder of marketing content. "It's on the server" or "It's on SharePoint" are the worst sentences you can hear when looking for a particular asset. If these collections aren't organized and maintained by someone with a structured mind, these places turn into landfills. Yeah, it's in there somewhere, but good luck finding it.

This is where a Digital Asset Management (DAM) comes in.

In addition to creating brand style guides, Brandfolder also has DAM capabilities. This is a system where all your assets are housed in one location and are searchable for easy access. There are tons of DAM vendors, such as Bynder, Acquia DAM (formerly Widen), or Optimizely DAM (formerly Welcome, formerly NewsCred). Many of your big MarTech ecosystems, such as Adobe, have DAM offerings, too.

As you can see from the names, there has been a lot of acquisition and consolidation in this space because there hasn't been much innovation over the past 20 years. AI has helped, but for the most part, it's just a database that displays assets.

If you have a smaller team and/or budget, Canva has the functionality to let people create their own branded assets within brand guidelines. Canva allows your creative team to lock down colors, fonts, image treatments, and much more. You can also build approval processes into the system. This way, someone from the brand or creative team would have to review and approve an asset before it could go out into the wild.

The goal of all these systems is to create on-brand content and then distribute it. Creating the content is one type of challenge. Distributing and maintaining the content is a completely different challenge. It's important to know that the same tools (or people) may not be best for addressing all of your needs.

Your branded assets could be the first exposure a prospect has to your business, products, or services. We all know the saying about first impressions. Now, what about the second impression? Or the third? If you want to be taken seriously, you must be consistent with every impression. One of the easiest ways is to have established visual brand standards and always follow them.

It's that simple.

When was the last time you evaluated your brand style guide? You don't have to wait for a rebrand to define how your visuals are used. Is your style guide publicly available on your website? People have different feelings about making this available to anyone, but my take is it helps to ensure that external parties are aware of what they should do when creating visuals with your brand identity. Even a simple style guide with only the essential pieces (brand voice, logo usage, typography, image treatment, etc.) will allow you to scale your work by empowering external partners to create on-brand visuals on your behalf.

Exploring your brand style guide will probably lead to exploring the content you've already created.

Visual Cues

- Your visual brand identity is one of your business's most valuable marketing assets.
- You have to answer a lot of questions before creating your visual brand.
- A brand is so much more than a logo.
- A brand is every interaction your customers and prospects have with your products, services, and business.
- As your product offerings evolve, you will need to evolve your visual marketing.
- It's possible to "own" a brand color, but it takes a lot of dedication to repetition.
- 69-90% of a consumer's initial judgment is based on color.
- Typefaces and fonts are different things.
- Brand guidelines help keep everyone on the same page when it comes to the visual brand.

CHAPTER 9:

Leveraging Existing Assets

"If Taylor Swift can re-record & release her old music, you can revise & reshare your old content."

—*Chantelle Marcelle*

You've spent a ton of time, money, and energy creating content that your audience loves. Now you just have to keep doing that until you die, right?

Wrong.

The dirty secret behind successful content creators is they use existing assets to make new assets.

And it's not really a secret. If you pay attention to the content successful people and businesses create, you'll see patterns. These creators understand how much it takes to produce a new asset. With limited time, money, and energy, they have to find new ways to scale their content and marketing efforts. They understand their audience, have established visual guidelines, and an understanding of their competitors. They've done all the hard work already.

Moz, the SEO marketing platform, repurposes its blog content into other formats, such as webinars, infographics, social media posts, and more. By leveraging high-performing blog posts, Moz can extend the life of its content and reach new audiences across different platforms.

Repurposing existing content is an easy way to stretch the lifespan of an asset. Think of it as making a stew out of the leftovers. Take what you have, repackage it, and serve it up again.

There are pieces of these assets that can be diced up and presented in new ways for audiences that may have missed your original asset. You did most of the hard work creating the asset initially; now is the time to get as much visibility as possible. These people want to see what you created, but they may not like the original content type.

Auditing your current visual content inventory

Before you start repurposing content, you need visibility into your current content arsenal. This serves two purposes: It allows you to see what you have, and it shows you what you don't have. With the right type of content inventory system (as discussed in Chapter 8), you should be able to see the expanse of what you've already created.

Figure 71: Original joke by Ann Handley

We also talked about the importance of tracking the performance of your visual content: Knowing what has worked and what hasn't worked in the past. Obviously, you want to do more of the stuff that works and less of the stuff that doesn't.

This exercise of evaluating your content will also let you know what you should remove from circulation. If an email isn't performing well, remove it from your nurture campaign. Or if you have a video on your YouTube channel that is just taking up space, remove it so viewers can stay focused on the better-performing content. Even if you don't know why something worked well and something else didn't, your audience will tell you what worked based on their engagement.

Depending on the rate you create content, you'll want to do a content inventory at least once a quarter. Just like anything, the more familiar you are with a topic, in this case it's your content, you'll be able to make better, faster decisions about what should be done next.

Strategies for repurposing and refreshing existing content

I love the topic of repurposing or refreshing existing content for one simple reason: YOU DON'T NEED TO RECREATE THE WHEEL EVERY TIME.

Sorry, was that too much?

Some folks don't want to share content again because "everyone already saw it." The first book printed on the original Gutenberg Press, which is also the most published book in the world, hasn't been read by everyone (it's the Bible). Knowing this, I promise some people missed your most recent amazing eBook. You can share it again.

If you're worried about the people who have already seen your perfect eBook, it may be time to refresh the asset. Sometimes it just needs a fresh coat of paint. Sometimes it needs to be stripped down to the studs and rebuilt.

Refresh it

If you have data-driven content, refreshing it may be as simple as updating the numbers and slapping a new cover or featured image on the visual content.

Infographics are great for updating year after year. Whatever stats you shared last year have been updated this year. You don't even have to change the design—you could simply swap the colors, and it will feel brand new.

Collect it

Do you have a series of blog posts that have a connected topic? Why not pull those together and offer it as an eBook? It has the same content but a different format. It gives you a chance to reach out to the customers or prospects who missed it the first time. If you have a substantial marketing automation system, you could target the people who read one of the blog posts but not the others. Email them and tell them about your new eBook that expands on the subject matter they've already shown interest in.

Deconstruct it

Remember that hour-long webinar from last quarter? Split it up into snackable videos. With the rise of Instagram Reels, TikTok, and YouTube Shorts, people are hungry for entertaining and informative short videos. Later in this chapter, we'll walk through how to turn one piece of content into 80+ additional pieces.

Expand it

If you have a blog post that did well, turn that into a white paper. Or maybe a video series. If people liked it the first time, there's a good chance they want a deeper dive into the subject. I can't tell you how many Tweets (RIP Twitter) or LinkedIn posts I've written that later turned into blog posts, Infographics, or SlideShares (back when that was a thing).

Recycle it

Let's say you have a great concept, but it's old. Or it didn't perform as well as it should have. When this happens, it's a great time to redo the asset. It's not unique that a good concept, wrapped in a less-than-ideal presentation, can cause an asset to underperform.

Switching to a new content type can help. Do you have a white paper that should have been better received? Rewrite and design it as an eBook. Sometimes, the information is good but too dense for the target audience.

Think of your content like a house hunting. Some houses have "good bones." You just have to look beyond the wallpaper (the old visuals) and imagine the untapped potential.

Figure 72: Midjourney prompt: the family room of a house is being rebuilt. We can see the 2x4s on the walls.

The visual marketing content strategy

You have one great piece of content planned. Maybe it's timed to coincide with a product launch, a press release, or a big industry event. Either way, you have an asset that took a lot of time, money, and effort to produce. You have high expectations for it, as do your bosses, who want to see the return on the investment. In this example, let's say it's an eBook.

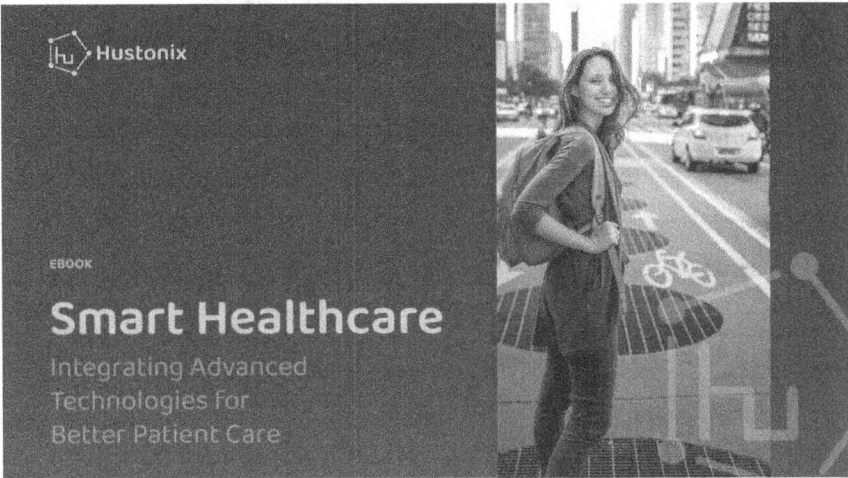

Figure 73: Hustonix 'Smart Healthcare' eBook cover

It would be great if your eBook were available in multiple languages at launch. If possible, it should also be customized for different verticals.

Figure 74: Hustonix eBook personalized by language and industry

Now you'll want to start slicing up the best of the content to share as teasers for different platforms.

The benefits of content recycling on SEO

Having multiple assets on the same topic helps tell Google and other search engines that you have authority on the topic. If these search engines notice a lot of content on one site, on one topic, and it gets traffic, it will help your page rankings.

Ryan Brock of DemandJump and co-author of the book Pillar-Based Marketing talks about the value that can be achieved by convincing Google you are the authority on a topic. He reports that after Google updated its ranking algorithm, clients that use pillar-based marketing saw a 22% increase in page one rankings.[1]

Recycling and refreshing your existing content allow you to have fresh content on a particular topic. If you can convince Google that you're the authority on that subject, it's a way to corner the market.

Having relevant content will also help you appear at the top of the Google results page. As of the writing of this book, this area is populated by the AI Overview. Before that, it was Snippets, the quick answers Google pulled from top sites and showed at the top of the results page.

SEO and Google are almost synonymous at this point. But things are rapidly changing in the world of search. AI is changing the whole game. For the sake of consumers and those who make content, we're all hopeful that Google will soon figure out what it wants to be after flailing around for the past couple of years.

The benefits of a content recycling approach to maximize ROI

Creating content takes time, money, and effort. The problem is you have a finite budget of time, money, and effort. What happens when you have to get more leads but don't have any more budget for copywriters? Or you have to increase traffic but only have three days before you have to start showing results? Or some other metric that lives outside the bounds of reality?

This is when you review your existing content pool and see what can be repurposed.

There was an initial investment of time, money, and effort in creating the original asset. Recycling, refreshing, or repurposing content allows you to get more out of that initial investment because you create more valuable content without needing to start from scratch. Would you rather swim 100 meters or 25 meters? Using existing content as your starting point is like shortening the race.

We're all under a time crunch. I worked with someone who had worked in Disney's interactive department, and he told me about their time constraints. It made me feel better that even employees at companies as big as Disney are under time constraints. That time crunch you feel is common. Knowing that time crunches are common for everyone, it's important to figure out where you can cut down on production time. Repurposing content cuts down on the time required to produce a new visual asset. Getting assets out to your audience faster increases the time that the asset is viable.

If you're using external contractors, the longer they spend to create an asset, the more expensive it is. And don't forget, your salaried employees also cost money. Those costs might come out of separate budget buckets, but it's still a cost. No matter who is creating the content, cutting down on the time to produce an asset cuts down on the cost. If you already have a lot of footage from an earlier video shoot, re-editing it to tell a slightly different story is going to be a lot cheaper than reshooting a completely new video.

The third ROI benefit I want to address is effort. This is usually ignored because it isn't tracked on a spreadsheet or calendar. It tends to be something the higher-ups don't consider. They tend to be more focused on putting a nickel into marketing and getting a dime out. But effort has a cost.

Effort is the x-factor for burnout. If people have to keep tapping into their creative well to create something new all the time, with ever-shrinking time and financial budgets, they will exhaust themselves. Once that creative well runs dry, it can be hard to replenish. There's a reason the expression "blood from a stone" exists. There is a mental—and sometimes physical—tax when it comes to creating something from nothing.

Having a well-performing asset is good, but what are the long-term implications if you burn out a great creative and then they quit? I'm sure we've all suffered various forms of burnout, so we know how damaging it can be to be pushed too hard. Don't underestimate effort when thinking about the ROI of recycling, refreshing, or repurposing existing content.

But what about AI? Can't we just use AI to repurpose content? Yes … but I wouldn't suggest it yet. It's not quite ready for prime time. It can be used for a first draft or some image generation, but low-effort content can easily be low-quality content. You don't want to damage your brand just to save time, money, or effort. It's only a matter of time until there's a tool that uses AI to create additional images based on an initial visual. It's just not there yet.

Innovative ways to transform traditional content into visual formats

One way to repurpose content is to identify the shortcomings of certain content and find new ways to present them. One example of this is podcasts. They're great for people on the go, but you can't easily skim a podcast. Any time you try to jump around by hitting the 30-second-skip button, it takes a few seconds to re-orientate yourself. Who knows what the host is talking about if you hit that 30-second button five or six times?

For a year and a half, I took highlights from podcasts and turned those stats into infographics. I found a way to take an audio-only asset and present it in a visual way. This allowed potential listeners to skim the information and determine if they wanted to spend 30-60 minutes to dive deeper into the information.

This could also work for webinars or videos. Creating static visuals with the key points in a video saves the viewer time. Items like this not only prove you are an expert on a topic, but they also show that you're willing to be helpful and present the content in a way they want to consume.

If you have a popular blog post, create a video talking about it. Marketing analytics and AI trailblazer Christopher Penn does this with his *Almost Timely* newsletter. After he's done writing it, he records a video of himself reading the newsletter. He then posts the video to YouTube and the audio as a podcast. This gives Chris' audience the ability to consume the content the way they like best. Three pieces of content are created out of one asset! Not only is he building his newsletter subscribers, but he's also building YouTube subscribers. Plus, having his thought leadership content discoverable on multiple platforms helps his SEO.

It's only a matter of time until AI technology and pricing models catch up with Chris' vision and allow him to automate his content into additional platforms easily.

Watch This Newsletter On YouTube 📺

Click here for the video 📺 version of this newsletter on YouTube »

Click here for an MP3 audio 🔊 only version »

Figure 75: Christopher Penn video embedded into the web version of his newsletter

Different people consume content in different ways. Whenever you can serve content in the format they want to consume, it shows you're taking them into consideration. It takes a little bit more time, but the results are win-win.

Tools for content repurposing and creative adaptation

There are some digital asset manager (DAM) systems that will crop images for you based on popular social media or website image sizes. The best ones will let you find the center point and crop around that space. This helps when you have a person in an image and want to ensure they don't get cut off by an edge.

This is a good use case for generative AI tools. You can feed your content into your GPT of choice and ask it what could be created from the existing asset. Once it provides that list, ask it to start telling you what to cut and what to keep for different content types. It probably won't do a great job with creating visual content, but it could give you snackable copy for social media, or maybe timestamps for video editing to create something new.

When recording a podcast episode, run a couple of cameras. Some people like to watch podcasts on YouTube or Spotify (I'm guilty of this for some podcasts). There are AI software tools out there that will help edit your podcast and video. Descript will do this plus create a transcript you can then run through a system like ChatGPT to make a blog post and/or a newsletter. And Descript clips your video into short vertical videos based on your prompt with the click of a button.

Content repurposing and expansion

In Figure 76, you'll see how you can take one piece of content and expand it to 80 different deliverables. It starts with one main pillar piece of visual content. Following this methodology allows you to reach out to your audience multiple times to engage them with the survey, see the survey results, and dive deeper into the insights that come from the industry survey.

These survey results help prospects prove to their leadership that this is an industry-wide problem everyone is trying to solve. It gives them the opportunity to say, "I'm not the only one with this problem, and here's who can help us solve it." As we know, executives love data-based decisions.

This also follows the "money follows pain" method of marketing. If you show people their pain (survey and survey results) and then reveal the solution to their pain (the pillar content that has a loose tie to your product or service), you'll be able to build trust because you've shown you understand your prospect's pain points.

This also helps with product development because prospects and customers tell you about their problems. Helping the product team is always a good thing.

Timeline	Day -30	Day -10	Day -5	Day -4	Day -3	Day -2	Day 0	Day 1	Day 2	Day 3	Day 4	Day 5	Day 10
Deliverable	Survey	Survey results					Content						Content webinar
Blog	Survey blog post	Results blog post						Blog post					
Add'l Deliverables													
			Vertical 1 blog post	Vertical 2 blog post	Vertical 3 blog post			Vertical 1 blog post	Vertical 2 blog post	Vertical 3 blog post		
			Results infographic					Content infographic					
Social 1	LinkedIn post		LinkedIn video		LinkedIn carousel			LinkedIn video			LinkedIn carousel		
Social 2	Instagram post		Instagram video	Instagram Reel	Instagram carousel			Instagram video	Instagram Reel		Instagram carousel		
Social 3	Threads/X post		Threads/X video		Threads carousel			Threads/X video			Threads carousel		
Social 4	Facebook post		Facebook video					Facebook video					
Video	Loom video		YouTube video	YouTube Shorts	TikTok video			Loom video	YouTube video	YouTube Shorts	TikTok video		
Email	Email		Email	Email (vertical)	Email (vertical)			Email	Email (vertical)	Email (vertical)			Email
Paid	Paid search/social – Survey/Survey results						Paid search/social – Content		Paid search/social – Webinar				

Language 1	Language 2	Language 3	Language 4	Language 5	Language 6
Vertical 1	Vertical 2	Vertical 3	Vertical 4	Vertical 5	Vertical 6

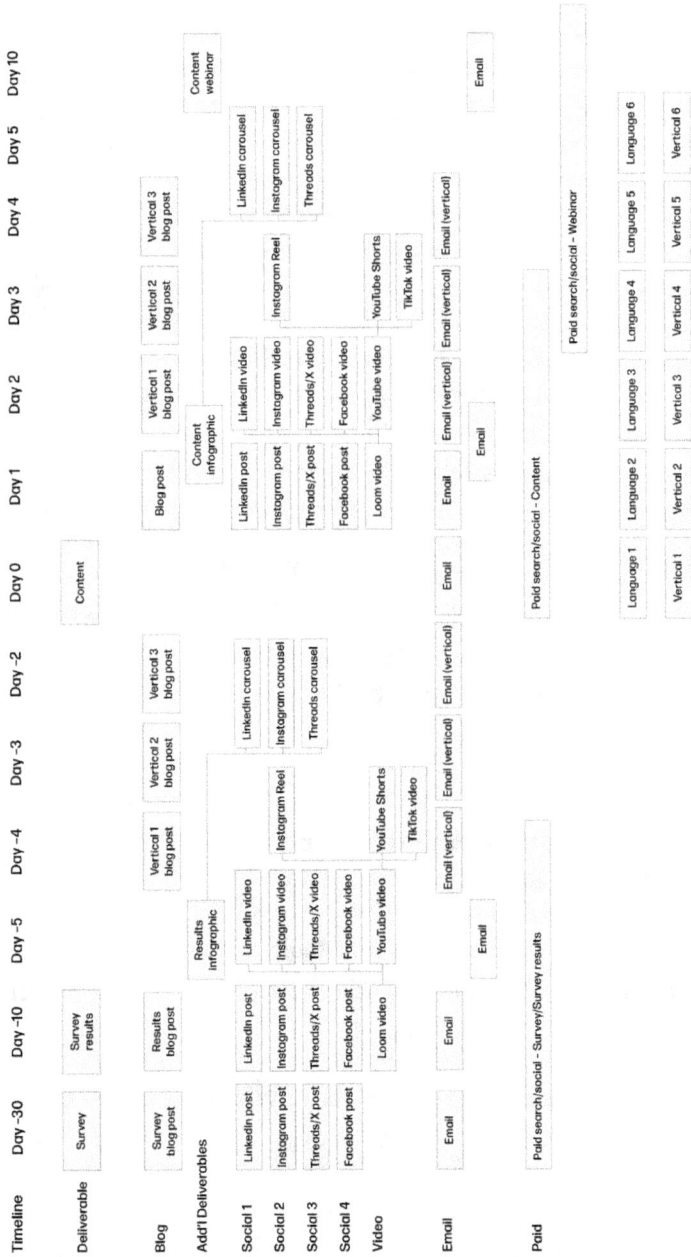

Figure 76: Pillar content roadmap

Examples of successful content repurposing strategies

Cathy McPhillips, chief growth officer at the Marketing AI Institute, is the reigning champion when it comes to using AI to repurpose podcast content. For every podcast the team produces, they also get four YouTube videos, four blog posts, five short-form videos (at least), and nine social assets.[2]

Years ago, Buffer, a tool that helps you publish content to different social channels, ran a "no new content" challenge with its team.[3] The goal was ONLY to repurpose content that had already been created. This led the team to take old blog posts and create new email drip campaigns based on that content. They also republished content to external blogging sites like Medium. Some things were as simple as refreshing old blog posts with updated information and imagery. New content like eBooks and courses could be built with existing content. They also created infographics, Pinterest images, and video content based on blog posts. The best part is the results were almost all positive!

Repurposing existing content is one of the best shortcuts to success. You put so much time, money, and effort into creating the original asset. Milk it for all its worth. If you're getting the results you want, find new ways to leverage that content.

There's no way your entire addressable audience has seen everything you've produced. There's a good chance YOU haven't even seen all the content your business has produced.

You should be able to get more out of your hard work than just more hard work.

Visual Cues

- Creating content takes time, money, and effort–get as much as you can from it.

- Successful content creators use existing assets to make new assets.

- It's like making a stew out of the leftovers: Take what you have, repackage it, and serve it up again.

- Before repurposing or recycling content, you need to know what is working or not working.

- Ways to repurpose your content

  ◦ Refresh it

  ◦ Collect it

  ◦ Deconstruct it

  ◦ Expand it

  ◦ Recycle it

- You don't need to recreate the wheel every time!

CHAPTER 10

A Beginner's Guide to Design Tools

"A good tool improves the way you work. A great tool improves the way you think."

—Jeff Duntemann

So, how do you create the content you want to share? There is more than one way to crack a nut. There are so many tools out there that it can be overwhelming to dig into.

When it comes to creating visual content, Adobe is the default name in the business. There's a reason that Photoshop is a proper noun as well as a verb. We've been "Photoshopping" images since the late 1980s. Personally, I started using Photoshop in the mid-'90s. I still remember my Desktop Publishing 1 teacher telling us that Photoshop now had layers so we could edit our files non-destructively (we've come a long way since cutting-edge features like that).

But what about the people who don't have 20-30 years of experience using these tools? For a long time, it was challenging to create engaging visuals without years of experience and/or paying someone with those skills.

In this chapter, let's explore the types of tools that anyone can use with minimal training and even less time to learn some of the more complex tools. In Chapter 13, we will dive into the pro-level tools.

Luckily, there are now tools that let anyone put together their visual packages.

Terms you should know before creating your visual content

Before we get much deeper, I want to clarify a few terms.

Vector file

These are line-based files. These files are made of points and lines in relationship to each other. These can scale to any size without the fear of losing resolution. The example I always use is that you could scale your vector logo the size of the moon and it will still be sharp.

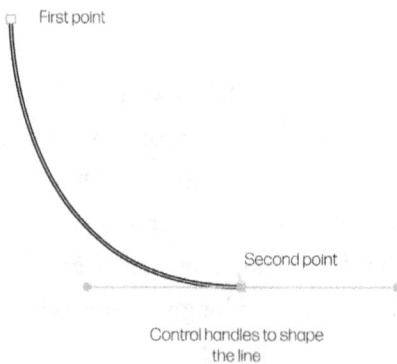

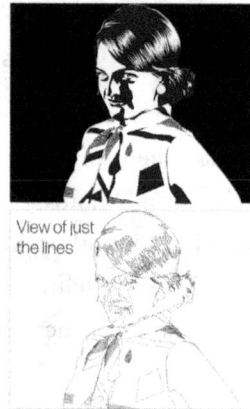

Figure 77: Vectors are points connected by lines

Raster images

These are pixel-based images; images that are made of tiny squares of different colors. The resolution is based on how many pixels your image has.

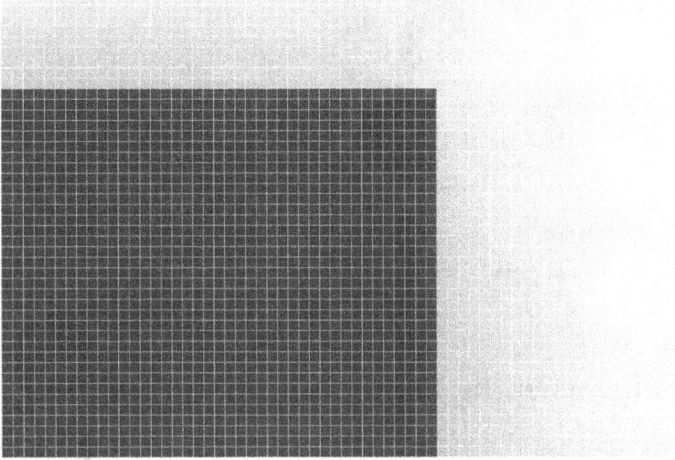

Figure 78: Raster images are pixel based

Video files

While you can include vector files in your working video files, the final output is more like a raster file built with pixels.

Popular DIY design software

Canva started as an alternative to PowerPoint and has expanded to include many new tools for creating different visuals. Canva has a massive user base and continues to grow. Canva's 2024 purchase of the Affinity suite of design tools has created the first real challenger to Adobe in the visual space in a long time.

Affinity's creative suite includes:

- Affinity Designer: Vector-based editing software
- Affinity Photo: Photo (raster-based) editor software

- Affinity Publisher: Page layout software

If you're looking for user experience software, the current leader is Figma. A few years ago, there was a shootout between Figma, Sketch, and Adobe XD, but that fight is pretty much over. Adobe abandoned XD during its failed acquisition of Figma, and Sketch is having trouble innovating at the same clip as Figma. Sketch and XD still work, but it looks like Figma will take this race.

Criteria for selecting the right tools for your objectives

Each of these tools has a set of features; some are stronger than others. Because each tool has an array of features, there is some duplication. When you're starting out, it can be hard to tell which tool should perform a specific task. With experience (or a few well-worded online searches), you can find which tool should be used for which task. Just because a tool can do a task doesn't mean it's the right tool to perform it. It's like the adage: Sure, you could use a hammer to drive a screw, but a screwdriver will work better.

It's likely you'll need a suite of tools that allow your team to create vector, raster, and video files.

The process gets much faster as you use the tools and learn the right one to use at the right time. Could this book have been created in Microsoft Word? Technically, yes, but it wouldn't have been as good. I had to use a variety of tools for the layout and images.

DIY graphics and visual creation

Canva is the default name in DIY graphics creations. There is a whole generation of marketers who are growing up with the ability to create visuals without needing designers. And some of these actually look good.

There are whole businesses that have been built to empower marketers to do more with Canva. With the right templates and brand assets, marketers can create eye-catching visuals.

Adobe Express (previously known as Adobe Spark) is another tool that lets anyone create branded visuals. The free version of Adobe Express provides templates you can easily edit in a web browser. You can change colors, text, and images for a poster. Or create an Instagram post based on one of the templates. You can mix and match your own imagery with the elements Adobe provides. It's amazingly simple.

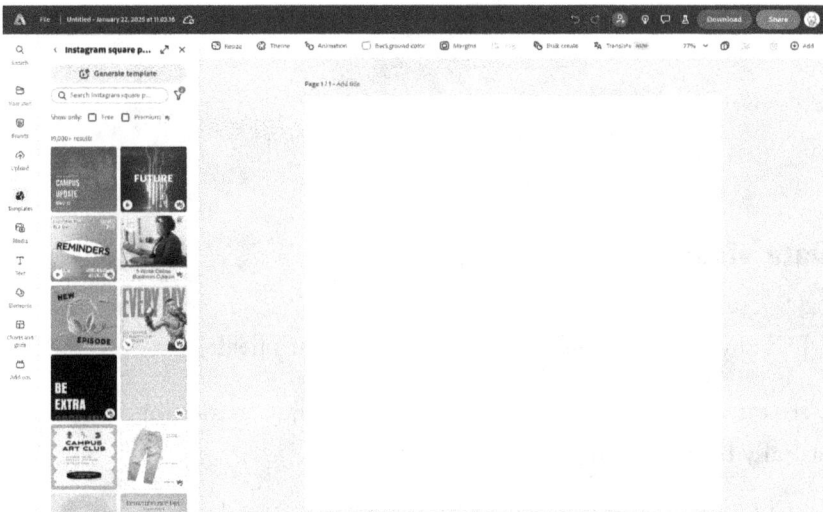

Figure 79: Adobe Express workspace

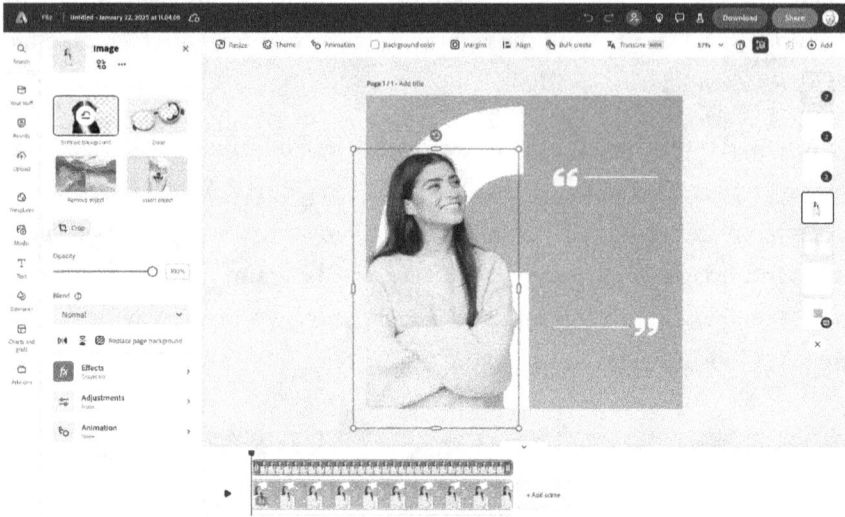

Figure 80: Adobe Express example

Data visualization tools

Did anyone warn you that marketing is a math field?

If you don't like numbers, you may not enjoy marketing. Marketing basically breaks down into three phases:

- Planning
- Execution
- Measurement

Two of those stages can include a lot of math … if you're doing it right.

Now that you're okay with math and combing through lots of data, let's figure out how to use those data-organization skills to create marketing assets. One of the best use cases of visual marketing is creating easy-to-consume data visualizations.

Whether you're creating an infographic, a set of slides, or a dashboard, there are tools out there that empower you to create visuals based on data. If you want to build dashboards, data aggregator tools like Tableau or Qlik can easily create visualizations once the data sources are connected to the tool.

If you're looking to spice it up a bit, Tableau will let you create interactive visualizations of data to engage the audience and drive them to additional content.

Tools like Infogram (now a part of Prezi) can also create static and interactive infographics, if you're looking to create infographics. These types of tools can help you create top-of-funnel infographics or lead-generation tools like online calculators. With a tool like Ceros, you can design an interactive quiz that allows visitors to answer some questions with the end result being the answer to a problem they're experiencing. When you put a lead generation form before the final answer, it entices the visitor to give you their contact information in exchange for the answer to their problem.

Then again, there's always good old Excel and PowerPoint. Since you're tracking content performance in Excel or some other repository, you can create graphs or other visuals within Excel and PowerPoint based on the content. Using your brand colors, you should be able to make some charts that are on-brand and show how well your content is performing.

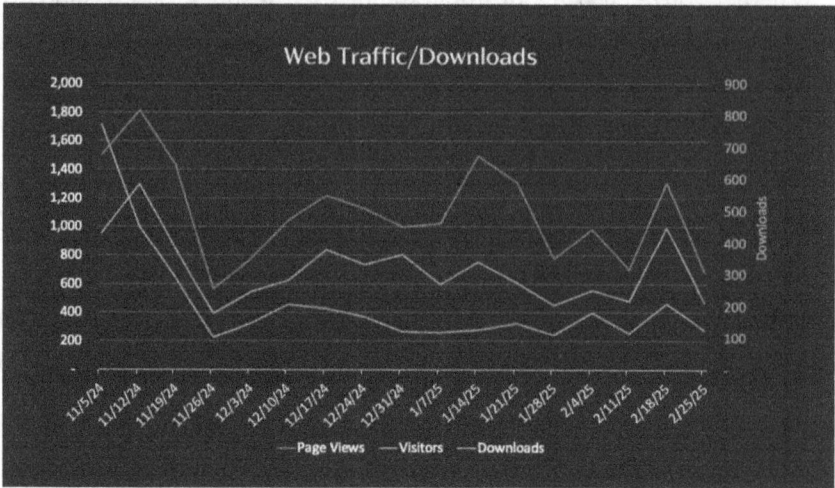

Figure 81: Example of on-brand dashboard

Video marketing tools

We're about a decade into the all-video-all-the-time phase of marketing. First, it was YouTube, and then Snapchat and Vine on social (don't get me started on the squandered opportunity that was Vine). Now it seems like all social apps are video apps. These sites want you to spend more time on them, and video is the easiest way to stop people from scrolling. They want you to stop to watch the video because, unlike text or an image, you can't easily skim video.

At this point, it's almost hard to remember when we didn't all have professional-grade video cameras in our pockets. These days, anyone can shoot video. And I can't count how many apps are available for video editing on my phone. Should I use CapCut (TikTok's video editor) or Meta's Edits app? Or how about Adobe Premiere Rush or Adobe Express, Adobe's limited-feature mobile and desktop apps that allows anyone to edit and share videos for free? I use an iPhone, so I also have access to iMovie if I want to edit videos right on my phone. There are so many options out there.

If you really want to get crazy, you can make videos out of 3D models using Blender or any number of modeling tools. I use Blender for these types of videos because it's one of the best 3D tools out there (and it's free). Be warned, though; there is a high barrier to entry before you can effectively use 3D modeling software. Thinking in three dimensions can be a little disorientating if you've only thought about the 2D space in the past.

Video is so important to so many audiences. Using some of the above tools, you should find ways to repurpose your existing, successful content into video form.

Chandler Quintin, co-founder and executive producer of The Video Brothers agency, an agency that has worked with companies such as LEGO, Google, Bose, and many more, gave some tips on how to get started with video:

> *"Creating your own content can be daunting, but as more and more professionals are diving into the 'content sphere' on social networks, it's almost a requirement that you 'know enough to be dangerous.' Before you go bananas, take a breath and realize that we all have to start somewhere.*
>
> *My best advice is to get behind the idea that simply starting will put you on the path to continually improve your output and process - and the rest will follow. To make content in general, you have a lot to think about... the content subject matter, the content itself, how you'll film it, where you'll film it, when you'll film it... and of course, how it will turn into a piece of content, and not raw footage. Here are some quick recommendations on how to get into content without breaking the bank:*
>
> ***Camera:*** *I always recommend starting your content journey by simply using the amazing smartphone you likely have in your pocket. Most of these devices shoot in 4k, look amazing, and plug right into on-board editing software or are easily ported to Adobe— and for those beginners out there, Adobe Rush is one of the easiest tools*

to use. *Pro Tip: If you're using an iPhone, use the rear camera for better quality, and AirPlay your device to a laptop so you can see and frame your shot. The front-facing camera is usually lower quality - although you can see yourself, it doesn't look as good.*

Audio: *Most phones will capture crystal clear audio - but, it might be hard to punch up when it comes to editing, and oftentimes, the devices capture a lot of ambient noise. A simple external mic that's compatible with Bluetooth or plugs into your device is ideal. A quick search on Google will have plenty of content creators giving reviews on the best microphone to use. It could be a podcast mic, a lavalier mic, or a small clip-on device. Regardless of how you do it, having a clean audio track of your voice is key. You'll offload the audio file to pair with your video file - Pro Tip: right when you press record on your video device and audio device, give a nice solid CLAP so you can sync audio and video accurately.*

Lighting: *Lighting is an art, for sure - but without extra lighting equipment, you can still look great on camera. Try to capture yourself with natural light that's going in your direction if you don't have any lights. For under $100 on Amazon, you can get ancillary LED lights and stands that you can set up to light yourself better. For less than that, you can get a ring light. The key to lighting is to make sure the lighting source is consistent and balanced. There are plenty of DIY lighting strategies you can find on YouTube which can take things from basic 1-light or natural light to slightly advanced 3-point lighting techniques. The fun thing about lighting is you can play around with what you have— background lights make a scene more vibrant, or turning your overhead lights off might give you a more serious mood.*

Post Production: *For anyone who wants a desktop experience for editing, I always point people to Adobe Rush, as it's not only so easy to use but there's plenty of DIY content around how to use the software very well. It's easy to learn and can be accessed across all of your devices. In your post software, you'll want to be able to add music, adjust audio* *levels, make cuts and edits, and tune the color slightly. Most of the beginner-based software have presets that make all of this very easy.*

For under $200, you can get what you need to make some seriously great content. For less than that and with what you have, you can make great content, too. The point is, don't get caught up in who's using what or this or that recommendation… your goal is to make great content, and that all starts with the subject matter you're putting into it.

As you enter your content journey, just remember that it doesn't need to be award-winning to be effective. Also, remember that practice makes perfect. The more you produce, the more you'll find areas to improve on - from the pre-production process through how you manage your editing."

Social media visualization

You can't talk about video without talking about social media. As I mentioned in the beginning of the last section, most social media apps are now primarily video apps because they want to capture and hold viewer attention. It helps these apps sell advertising because of the average time on site.

Many of the top apps have built-in visual creation tools. I'll admit to firing up Instagram just to mess around with an image before texting it to someone. The same can be done for social media images or videos.

And we can't talk about social media visualizations without mentioning memes. It's half the reason we scroll social media. Those fun images or gifs with something clever written on them in bold white type (the typeface is called Impact) with a black border. Just like the unlimited number of video apps available for phones, there are just as many meme generators.

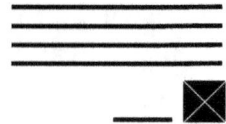

Figure 82: Drawing of Success Kid meme

If you find yourself in a pinch, fire up Giphy and run a search. Most of the gifs and memes you can think of are ready to be shared with your audience, if your audience is into that sort of thing. If you're marketing life-or-death pharmaceuticals, maybe don't use the Crying Jordan meme.

Together
we're stronger than
Hangnails

Figure 83: Drawing of Crying Jordan meme

Use the right visual tool

As mentioned earlier, you don't want to use a hammer if you're trying to drive a screw. Using the right tool for the right task can make all the difference. Sure, you could use PowerPoint for your data sheets, but is the result actually good for the end user?

The answer to that rhetorical question is "no." Avoid creating graphics that look like they were produced in PowerPoint. Your audience is most likely familiar with PowerPoint graphics, and you want to produce something better than the average person.

The person consuming the content is more important than the person producing the content.

Over a decade ago, I worked with a team of product marketing managers who wanted to use Microsoft Publisher for their data sheets. I don't know what the proposed use case was when Microsoft Publisher was developed, but I can't imagine it was for creating customer-facing content. Combine a non-design tool with people who don't understand design, and you can imagine how poorly these assets turn out. The bad text flows, images appearing on the wrong page, and giant blocks of white space between paragraphs. It was unprofessional, to say the least.

Luckily, we hired a new VP of product management from one of our much larger competitors. He admonished his team for not using our in-house design resources to produce these critical documents. He told them that nobody would take our products seriously if our collateral looked like a mom-and-pop shop produced it.

More companies need leaders who understand the importance of well-crafted visual marketing assets. Even if the difference between professional and amateur design may not be visible to you, your customers and prospects will inherently know the difference.

Canva is doing a lot to help marketers create and edit their own marketing content. If you work with a brand team or designers, they can help set up templates and lock down brand elements within the Canva templates to ensure the content being produced is on brand. If you don't have access to an in-house creative team or regular contractors, I highly suggest investing in a professional to help set up your Canva environment before you get started. Those visual brand guidelines will help you in ways you may not realize.

Feature	Adobe Creative Cloud	Canva
Price	Multiple pricing tiers based on apps, requires individual subscriptions for each team member	Free plan, Pro, and Teams plans unlock premium content and features
Learning Curve	Steeper, designed for professionals with advanced tools	Easy to use, intuitive drag-and-drop editor, minimal learning curve
Templates	Limited templates available via Adobe Stock or external files	Thousands of ready-made templates included, especially with Pro plan
Photo Editing	Advanced photo editing with Photoshop, including RAW file support	Basic photo editing, lacks advanced features like RAW processing
Typography	Access to 30,000+ typefaces via Adobe Fonts	1,300+ typefaces, with more available for premium users, basic text effects
Stock Photos	Requires additional Adobe Stock subscription	Pro plan includes more than 1 million stock assets

Feature	Adobe Creative Cloud	Canva
File Formats	Supports JPEG, PNG, EPS, SVG, PDF, TIFF, MP4, etc	Supports JPG, PNG, PDF, PPT, GIF, MP4
Non-Design Tools	Primarily design-focused	Includes non-design tools like content planner, translation, print services

The same applies to Adobe Express and a variety of other consumer tools. Finding a designer or brand manager to help you set up these tools will put you miles ahead of where you'd be if you tried to do it yourself.

The tools matter less than the final output. But if you're not using the right tools, it can be difficult to get the right output.

Visual Cues

- Three file types to know:
  - Vector files
  - Raster files
  - Video files
- Play with the different tools available to you so you know which tool is best for different tasks.
- Compare and contrast Adobe Creative Cloud vs. Canva.
- The person consuming the content is more important than the person producing the content.

CHAPTER 11

The Visual Content Spectrum

"A wealth of information creates a poverty of attention."

—*Herbert A. Simon*

It's true. There is simply too much content out there. There is no way to pay attention to all of it. How does the average consumer know what to consume? It's not like there is some Netflix-style algorithm to tell someone what marketing content they should consume.

That's where you come in. You will create visual content that not only captures attention but also engages and entertains your prospects, and customers and, ultimately, benefits your business.

Right?

Of course you will! But with so many different types of visual marketing content, where will you begin?

Comprehensive exploration of various visual content types (images, videos, infographics, etc.)

So, what exactly is "content"?

Figure 84: Drawing of One Does Not Simply ... meme

Content is a fancy word for stuff. It can mean almost anything at this point.

Marketing content is the stuff you or your business creates to attract, engage, and retain an audience.

Visual marketing content highlights the content through the use of images, videos, illustrations, or other pieces of multimedia content, to further attract, engage, and retain an audience.

Let's take a few minutes to discuss some different types of visual content. For the next few pages, we'll stay focused on B2B marketing content. Remember, you don't have to do all of these. It's way too much for a few people, let alone just you, to create.

Print Advertisement

What they are

These are visual marketing messages to help promote a product, service, or brand. These ads are printed on a material, like a magazine or newspaper.

What they do

These advertisements are mostly for brand awareness, but they can also serve as calls to action in some cases.

Because most print advertising lives until the piece is destroyed or taken down, and can be difficult to measure for effectiveness, using these for performance marketing (marketing you can measure) can be a significant challenge. The idea is to keep your product or service top of mind for when the prospect enters your market. The viewer may not be in the market for your product or service right now. The goal is that when the viewer suddenly needs a product or service like yours, you are the first one s/he thinks of.

Think of all the ads you see for engagement rings. The ads are often a view of the beautiful ring or a woman's hand with a ring on it, silhouetted on a black background. Elegant typography accompanies this striking image. This is (hopefully) a one-time purchase for people, but since there is no way to target these people at the right time, jewelry companies must constantly advertise so they're top of mind when it comes time to pop the question.

A scenario where brand and performance marketing cross is automobile dealerships.

Think of a car ad on Memorial Day weekend. Car dealers will often run advertising to promote a deal during a holiday weekend. The ad has a call to action that hopefully compels the viewer to take immediate action

Why you should use them

Though the print medium has had a couple of rough decades, there is still a dedicated audience that consumes printed materials.

Visual tips

Printed materials are printed in CMYK or black and white. This means it's tougher to use bright, neon colors to grab attention. In many publications, your advertisement will appear on the page on the right. This is because it is seen the longest. When the person reads from the front of the magazine or newspaper, as they flip the pages, the right page is in view longer than the left page. Knowing you have the viewer's undivided attention for a second means you must design something that keeps their attention rather than attracts it. Use visuals like people's faces or bold typography to keep the viewer engaged. If you're looking to measure engagement, try adding a QR code to entice the viewer to go to a digital platform to learn more or take further action.

Digital advertisement

What they are

Advertisements that live within a digital space, such as a website or application. You can't escape them, no matter how many ad blockers you install on your browser. Because wide swaths of the internet are ad-supported, most websites have advertising on them.

What they do

These rectangular images or videos are used for the same purposes as print advertising (to attract, engage, and retain an audience). Still, they're more likely to try to get the viewer to take action right then and there. Digital advertisements can be set up to measure views, engagements, and other metrics you may be interested in knowing.

Why you should use them

These ads often try to get you to click because those clicks are measurable. Digital advertisements come with analytics far superior to those of print advertisements. For performance marketing teams, it's often important to show return on investment (ROI) with marketing efforts. If your marketing automation and customer-relationship management (CRM) platforms are aligned, you can measure the exact spend and attribute revenue back to those campaigns.

Because CMO tenure tends to be the shortest of the c-suite, many successful CMOs have learned that when they show results based on spend, they're more likely to keep their jobs. This makes digital advertising more valuable to the CMO and the organization as a whole because there is lower turnover.

Visual tips

The viewers don't want to see your ads. They are a distraction from the reason they are on a page or application. Your goal is to grab their attention and get them to do something they weren't planning on doing. These are often bright ads with motion that try to distract you from the reason you're on a particular web page. As we discussed in Chapter 2, our brains are wired to look at motion and movement. When creating these ads, you have to consider the potential environments in which they'll live. If your digital ad is going on a busy page, you don't want to add more visual noise to the viewer's screen.

Due to limited real estate, you have to grab attention quickly and hope that the user is less interested in the original reason they went to that page or app.

Infographic

What they are

A visual representation of data or information.

What they do

While not as popular as they once were, these visual assets are a great way to show data in an easy-to-consume way. Most infographics were traditionally static images, jpgs, pngs, or gifs. Lately, the trend has been using interactive infographics to engage the audience further and let them consume the content at their own speed.

Why you should use them

Prospects and customers like easy-to-consume information. Infographics are a great way to get information out there. It helps your business because it shows thought leadership. Creating and sharing assets like this builds trust and affinity because you're helping your prospects and customers improve their jobs.

Visual tips

These images can use photos, icons, illustrations, or any other static visual elements to help spotlight the data or information you want to display.

Infographics can follow your visual brand style or not. Creating off-brand infographics can be a good thing if you're talking about your industry. Branded content always has the air of vendor propaganda. When you create an off-brand infographic, it can feel more like an unbiased asset, even if it has your logo at the bottom.

People are more likely to share infographics that help people in their fields. People love to show off how smart they are. One of the best ways to do this is to share content you've consumed that others might enjoy and learn from. You can start to be seen as a thought leader or early adopter if you're constantly sharing useful information.

To empower these people who can share your content, make content that doesn't feel like vendor propaganda. For example, nobody is going to share a branded infographic that talks about the throughput of your new wireless access point product. But they'll share content that provides useful information about advancements in throughput in the Wi-Fi industry.

Webinars

What they are

Webinars are a type of online presentation where someone presents information to an audience.

What they do

Webinars allow a person or team to present information to large groups of people. Usually these are one-way conversations with the presenter speaking and showing slides to an audience who is unable to interact. Some webinars have a chat functionality that allows the audience to chat with other viewers as well as the presenters. This (mostly) one-way transfer of information helps keep the speaker on track during their presentation. You'll sometimes see a time for questions and answers at the end of the live webinar.

Why you should use them

Webinars are good for marketing because you can promote them twice: once as an upcoming live event and then again as an on-demand asset. After the live presentation has concluded, webinars are often added to resource centers, where other viewers can watch the pre-recorded webinar at their convenience.

Visual tips

Don't talk to your slides. Nobody wants to watch you read your boring slides. Create slides with imagery that helps people remember the point you were making. The right visual will help lock an idea into the viewer's mind. The goal is to transfer information, so the slides need to convey the information in a way that benefits the audience, not just the speaker.

Presentations slides

First, a point of clarification: I define slide decks and presentation decks as two separate things. Slide decks are for presenting information to an audience. Presentations can share information, but they're also inspirational and aspirational. Think of the best presenters you've seen. Did they have a bunch of white slides with 24-point black text on them? Were they telling you how a division did last quarter? Probably not. The best presenters are selling aspiration, and their visuals support this.

What they are

When a keynote presenter is on stage, they will often have slides displayed behind them. These slides should be clean, bright, and straightforward. You don't want the slides competing for attention with the speaker.

What they do

These slides reinforce what the speaker is saying. They're not just a script of the speaker's speech. It can be a few bullets designed in an interesting way that reinforces what the speaker is saying. Movies and TV are a combination of audio and video. These slides are the visual part of the speaker's talk track.

Why you should use them

Presentation slides can help drive home the points you're trying to make when speaking on a stage, especially a keynote stage. You want the viewer to walk away from the session having learned something. The right presentation slides will help you help the viewer.

Visual tips

You need to find a way to get your point across with the fewest words possible. Fewer words = bigger impact. There should be a lot of space around the copy to help spotlight what is important. Find imagery or design elements that tie an emotion to your point. Back in Chapter 2 we talked about the benefits of having emotionally triggering visuals. This is the time to really tap into the power that a large screen can have over a captive audience.

Most of these slides will be shown surrounded by a dark background. Play with colors to see which ones fit your brand and can still grab attention.

Videos

What they are

Video is a series of moving pictures, sometimes with audio attached to it, sometimes with text on the video.

What they do

Videos can be used for an array of use cases. As we've seen with social media over the past five years, many of these platforms are moving to video-first content. Videos can entertain, inform, or just help kill time.

Why you should use them

In a 2022 survey[1] of sales, marketing, and customer experience professionals, 82% stated that video is becoming more important to their business. If you're looking to drive conversions, video does well, with 70% reporting video as their best content for driving conversions. YouTube is one of the top websites for finding new information. Creating videos that appear on YouTube and other video-based platforms will help customers discover your brand or company.

Visual tips

For a long time, video had a high barrier-to-entry. The cost for the equipment, crew, and editing was prohibitive for many people or businesses. But now that we all have near-professional video and editing software in our pockets, it's possible for more people to produce high-quality video.

But they don't have to be high-quality. If your visual brand works with lower-quality, DIY-style video, you can create content faster and with less effort and money. Those walk-and-talk videos we see on LinkedIn perform well because they have a level of authenticity that over-produced videos don't have.

Social images/video

What they are

Static or animated images that accompany messages.

What they do

Help grab attention or reinforce the message being shared on the platforms where people are already spending time.

Why you should use them

Images or videos are necessary on some platforms, like Instagram or TikTok. On other platforms, like LinkedIn, Twitter/X, Bluesky, or Threads, it's possible to have text-only posts. But posts with images perform better. Data from Emplifi[2] reinforces that visual and video perform significantly better than simple text-based posts. Through six quarters, ending in Q4 2023, brand post interactions consistently went up across Instagram, TikTok, Twitter/X, and Facebook.

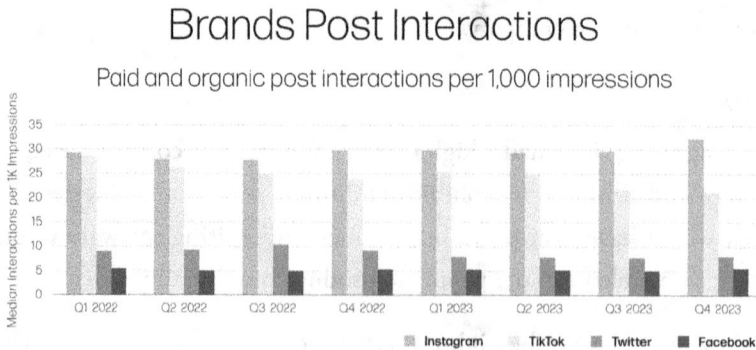

Figure 85: Brand post interactions

184

Visual tips

Video takes longer to consume than static content, so it makes sense that video performs better than static images because the platforms want viewers to spend more time there. Knowing this, figure out if there are ways to animate your static imagery to boost engagement and impressions.

Datasheet

What they are

PDFs (or on-page content) that give in-depth information on a product.

What they do

Provide deeper information on a company's product or service. These are usually consumed later in the buying process when the buyer is getting ready to make the final decision.

Why you should use them

Toward the end of the buying cycle, prospects compare statistics on similar products from different companies. A datasheet will help illustrate exactly what your product or service does.

Visual tips

These should be clean and easy to read. You already have the prospect on the hook. They want a deep dive into your product. Make it easy to consume. It should not be flashy. The information just needs to be well organized. Use tables where possible. For what it's worth, I don't have a strong opinion on whether datasheet should be one word or two.

White paper

What they are

A white paper is less about your products and more about something related to the industry.

What they do

White papers help people learn deeper industry news. After reading a white paper, the reader should be able to apply some of that knowledge to their job.

Why you should use them

There are two reasons why white papers are good visual marketing content: lead generation and showcase of expertise. The viewer should get the impression that the white paper is worth the cost of their email address (which they usually provide to access the white paper). The white paper should also be a way to illustrate to prospects that you are an expert in this particular area of interest.

Visual tips

These PDFs are usually pretty straightforward, text-heavy documents. You can decorate them a little, but for the most part, the pages should be clean with easy-to-read type. Use subheads and section titles to help the viewer understand where they are.

Make sure you use a typeface made for reading large amounts of copy. Serif typefaces work well. Also, it's not ideal to use black text on a white background. A dark gray will work better because it's easier on the eyes. You could use a dark mode color scheme, but if it's an asset that may be printed and distributed, dark backgrounds with light type can have printing issues, making the text harder to read, and expensive to use all that ink.

Blog post

What they are

A blog is a collection of written articles on your website on a topic related to you, your business, or your industry. A blog post is an individual article.

What they do

Blog posts help demonstrate expertise. Usually text based, a blog is a collection of blog posts that is used as an area to add new thought-leadership content to your website on a regular basis.

Why you should use them

In addition to showing off your knowledge, blog posts can help with search engine optimization (SEO). Having web pages dedicated to topics around your subject area lets the search engines know you are an authority on the topic and that people searching on this topic should visit your site.

Visual tips

Break up your text. Use imagery and pull quotes to give your viewers' eyes a chance to relax. Use headlines and subheads so the viewer can skip around if they want to. Using proper HTML formatting with these subheads will help search engines better understand and categorize your content.

eBook

What they are

An eBook is a digital document used to educate the audience on a topic related to your business. Usually, they are PDFs that are easy to read. They are higher-level content that is more visual than a white paper.

What they do

Marketing eBooks helps your business demonstrate areas of expertise that are of interest to your prospects and customers. They can focus on industry trends or a compilation of your most popular blog posts. It's a way to present content visually that is interesting and easier to consume.

Why you should use them

eBooks are quicker to produce and distribute than traditional books. These can be used for lead-generation campaigns by gating (a gate is another term for a form) the eBook and encouraging visitors to provide their email addresses or other contact info to read it.

Visual tips

This is where traditional print design skills cross with interactive design skills. When laying out an eBook, it should be easy to read like a magazine or book, but it can also have interactive elements baked into the pages. The cover should be so engaging it convinces viewers to read it.

Podcast

What they are

An audio recording of a conversation or a produced show.

What they do

Podcasts allow people to consume content while they're doing something else. It's one of the very few forms of content that encourages multitasking.

Why you should use them

Podcasts are one of the fastest-growing forms of content today. Though the industry isn't growing as much as it was in the early 2020s, it's still growing year over year.[3]

Podcast Listeners in the US

Share of Monthly Podcast Listeners (US Population 12+)

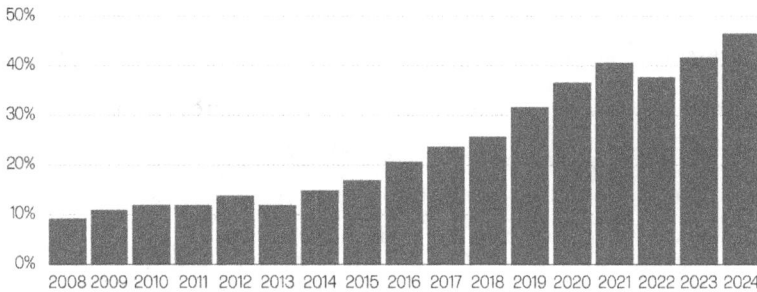

Figure 86: Podcast listener growth

Visual tips

Make sure you have a great thumbnail. Whether it's for your show over-all or a new image for each episode, eye-catching thumbnails are important. Because thumbnails are small (hence the name), yours must be as simple and straightforward as possible. Use contrasting colors, short words, and type that can be read quickly.

If you have a well-known thought leader or are in the process of building one up, put the host's photo on the thumbnail. You'll have to determine if that person's image is more recognizable than their name or show name. It's such a small area; make sure your image and type aren't fighting for attention.

Product Guide

What they are

These are essential product catalogs. It's a listing of all your business' products.

What they do

Product guides show customers and prospects the array of products that are available to them. If they're already a customer, it can show them solutions to their other challenges.

Why you should use them

No prospect only has one problem to solve. They are most likely looking to solve a particular problem when they come upon your business or marketing content. Showing them the full breadth of your capabilities could entice them to buy more than they originally planned.

Think of Amazon. While you're reviewing one product, there is always a "You might also like…" A product guide shows additional products likely to appeal to the prospect or customer.

Visual tips

Product guides must be laid out in a clean, obvious way. It needs to be obvious to the viewer how these products can work together. Do not organize your products based on how your business is organized. They don't care how your internal organization is structured. They care about solving their problems. Make sure you organize your products and offerings in this way.

Newsletter

What they are

Newsletters are emails from a brand that are released on a regular basis. They usually follow the same organizational structure in each issue. Different segments of the newsletter typically give an overview of a topic with a link to a web page.

What they do

These emails are informational and should focus on helping the reader. This is not the place for product pitches. It's about helping the reader and driving traffic to information they may have missed on your website or someone else's.

Why you should use them

Successful newsletters help build awareness and trust. People have built entire businesses with newsletters as the backbone. Newsletters are ideal for building an audience who has opted in to receive your information.

Visual tips

Train your readers to get accustomed to receiving helpful information regularly. Email is notoriously difficult to design because of the differences between email applications. Make sure you have sections of information so the reader can jump to relevant information. Images and colors can help denote different sections of the newsletter. Unlike a regular email, the purpose of a newsletter is to be helpful, not necessarily to drive viewers back to your website to get them to convert.

Sales deck

What they are

Slides created in PowerPoint, Canva, Google Slides, or some other application, that help the salesperson tell their story.

What they do

These decks help reinforce information that is being conveyed verbally to a prospect.

Why you should use them

Sales decks (or sales presentations) help prospects absorb the information so they can realize your product or service is the right solution to their problem.

Visual tips

These slides should have information presented in a clear, organized way. This is a transfer of information and should be designed differently than Presentation Slides. You can have design elements on there, but they should be secondary to the information.

I recommend having different decks for different stages of the conversation. For the initial meeting, the information is at a higher level. You're introducing the business and its expertise to the prospect. The second meeting should have a deck with deeper information. These slides can be a bit busier because the prospect wants to know more of the fine details.

Remember that salespeople like to customize their presentations, so make sure the slides are editable. If necessary, you could lock down the company-level slides, but remember that most salespeople are storytellers and like to craft stories in their own way.

Awareness handout (flyer)

What they are

These are assets that are the size of a typical piece of paper (8.5" x 11" in the U.S., A4 in the rest of the world). They will have printing on one or both sides. Sometimes they are folded into thirds and designed as a tri-fold handout.

What they do

Flyers let the viewer walk away from a conversation with information to be consumed later.

Why you should use them

Instead of making the prospect consume all the information on the spot, handouts or flyers let the viewer peruse the content when the time is right for them.

Visual tips

This asset type can be a catch-all for any content you want to share. Sometimes, there is a request or need for an asset that doesn't fit into pre-existing categories. For many content types, using pre-built templates can save time and energy. Because the content on flyers tends to be flexible, the design can also be flexible, depending on the need.

Poster

What they are

Posters are printed assets, usually flat sheets of paper, that promote high-level information. Sizes can range from 11" x 17" (or A3) to 24" x 36" (or A1) or larger.

What they do

Transfer basic information as succinctly as possible. These are made to capture the attention of people who aren't necessarily looking for your information.

Why you should use them

Posters, when properly designed, force the viewer to see them and consume their basic information. They're large and, when they stand out from the surrounding area, can be hard to miss.

Visual tips

There are thousands of books written on poster design (I have many of them). The goal is to get the basic information across as clearly and quickly as possible in an eye-catching way. Posters can be used for anything from teasing an upcoming product release to your band's gig on Friday night.

Bookmark

What they are

Small pieces of thick paper that hold your place in a physical book.

What they do

Hold a reader's place in their book.

Why you should use them

Creating branded bookmarks allows you to stay top of mind whenever someone is reading their book.

Visual tips

Bookmarks can be uses as brand or product/service assets. But think about the long-tail of this asset. Some readers hold on to bookmarks for years. If you discontinue the product/service, do you still want people to see this bookmark when they're reading?

Live events/Trade shows

What they are

(Okay, these aren't technically content assets, but they're places where visual marketing can make a difference.) A booth within a trade show event. These booths will usually have some sort of backdrop, plus a table or other area(s) where you can show the value you provide.

What they do

At a trade show or other in-person event, you set up a booth to entice people to come into your area and learn more about what you do.

Why you should use them

Trade shows and live events are great ways to get in front of prospects in your target market. These events are tailored to a specific audience. If your audience will be attending, it's a good idea to put big signage in front of this audience promoting your business.

Visual tips

Exhibiting at an in-person event means you're probably stationed right next to a business looking to attract the same audience. Bold is the word you'll want to remember. Colors. Typography. Copy. It shouldn't be gaudy, but find ways to create large graphics that will make someone slow down as they are walking by.

The goal is to get them to stop and ask a question. Then, your booth people can engage with them further. If there's an offer or a guest speaker, that can help bring traffic to the booth. Swag is good, but you have to be okay with losing inventory to swag hags (people who want to collect free stuff).

Best practices for creating and utilizing each type of visual content

As you'll notice from the list above, there are many content types. Which type of content you create depends on your audience, products, and marketing plan. Do not start with the idea of creating a certain type of content. Start with the audience and determine what will work best for them. Too often, a marketing manager or someone higher up will say, "We should create an eBook." or, "Let's do a webinar next month," without fully thinking about the information they want to convey and the audience's needs.

Whatever you create, remember that everything should be visually consistent. They will look different because each asset serves a different purpose, but it should be obvious to the viewer that everything they see from your business was created with intention. They should be able to move from asset to asset without a feeling of confusion.

Consistent visuals establish a baseline of familiarity for the viewer. If they consumed something they enjoyed with your visuals, they will assume the next asset with similar visuals will be of similar quality.

The role of each content type in the marketing funnel:

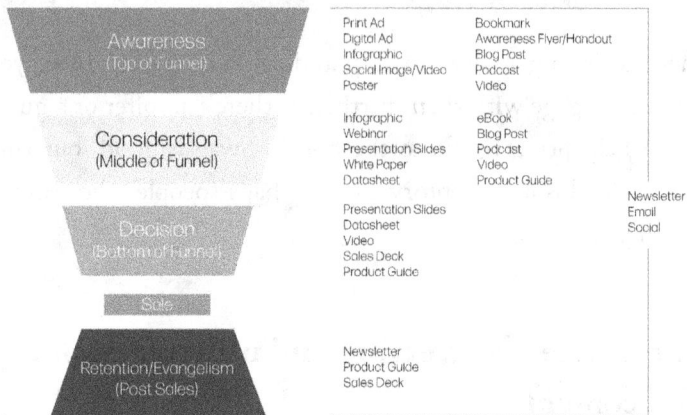

Figure 87: Sales/marketing funnel with content for each stage

Some asset types are used across different stages of the marketing funnel. The main thing to remember is that people need and want different types of information at different stages.

Early on, prospects are identifying an issue that needs to be solved. They've discovered a problem and now they need to find a solution. Your goal is to be there when the prospect is looking for a solution. During this awareness stage (also known as the top of the funnel), you want to share content that is high-level and demonstrates that you understand their problem.

Once they've established that a particular business understands their problem, the prospect will start to look for more information to see if the solution the business offers is the best solution for their problem. This is the consideration stage (middle of funnel) where they are weighing your solution against others who offer similar solutions. Your content should be providing deeper information about your solution and company. You're building trust at this stage.

Finally, the prospect will want proof that you have solved similar problems in the past. Case studies and use cases are ideal for proving you know how to solve the problem. This is where the prospect has determined that they are making the right choice by choosing your solution.

Much of the decision process comes down to "will I get fired if I buy this?" It's your job to remove those fears and get them to take action now. Based on the products your business produces, the biggest competition is often "doing nothing." Sticking to the status quo ruins more deals than any of your competitors.

Don't forget, we buy based on emotion and justify with logic. Michael Harris of Salesforce[1] conducted research to see if this old adage was true. It turns out, the answer is "kinda" (my term, not his). According to Harvard Business School professor Gerald Zaltman, 95% of purchase decisions take place unconsciously.

> "I discovered, for example, that people do not decide emotionally. The decision to buy is made subconsciously, and these subconscious decisions are based on a deeply empirical mental processing system that follows a logic of its own.
>
> Our subconscious/intuitive decision to buy is then communicated to the conscious mind via an emotion. The conscious mind then

searches for rational reasons, and that's how we complete the circle: We justify our emotional signals to buy with logical reasons."

—*Michael Harris*

Knowing this, make sure you're using the right balance of emotion and facts at the right points of your buyer's journey.

Also, when it comes to funnel stages, sometimes you'll see the terms TOFU, MOFU, and BOFU (Top of the Funnel, Middle of the Funnel, Bottom of the Funnel). I'll let you decide if you want to use these terms. I've found that it leads to more confusion and snickering when they're used in a business setting.

Trends in visual content creation

Trends will help tell you what type of content you should create. Trends are people telling you exactly what type of content they want to consume. If your prospects consume a lot of long-form video, create more of that. If they're reacting to memes, keep meme-ing!

At some point, the current trends will shift, and you'll have to shift your content production to follow them. Infographics were all the rage a decade ago. Now, not so much. Back then, nobody really cared about mobile video. Now everything is Reels, Shorts, and TikTok.

Everyone wants to be early on a trend, but this is difficult for any marketing team. One easier thing is knowing which content to stop producing. This is where checking your analytics, observing competitors, and talking to customers and prospects helps.

As for modern trends, that is constantly in a state of flux. Just know that the basics–clearly communicating your message and desired action–will always be trendy. Enable your audience to take the action you want them to take. Then you and your content have done your jobs.

While creating visual content, think about what your prospects want. There is so much noise out there. Ask yourself what will be useful for them. Or ask them what they want to see. You're trying to build awareness, affinity, and trust with your content. Make sure you're not just adding to the noise and creating more content just to create content.

Visual Cues

- You create marketing content to attract, engage, and retain an audience.
- Do not start with the idea of creating a specific type of content.
- Look through the list of content types to learn what they are, how they're used, and how to create effective versions.
- Start with the audience and determine what will work best for them.
- Consistent visuals establish a baseline of familiarity for the viewer.
- The viewer should be able to move from asset to asset without a feeling of confusion.
- We buy based on emotion and justify with logic.
- Because there is so much noise, think about what will be helpful for your audience.
- Don't add to the noise just to check a box.

CHAPTER 12

Visual Content Marketing Creation Guidelines

"Don't just grab attention. Hold it. Don't try to be 'relevant.'
Try to be their favorite."

—*Jay Acunzo*

You made it! There was a lot in that chapter. I'm sure you already knew parts of it. Thanks for making it this far. Now, let's dig into how to create visual content.

Your goal is to create content that people want to consume. Some content will feel like homework. Nobody wants that. You're not paid enough to create soul-crushing content that nobody will like or consume. You need to create visual content that viewers will enjoy and learn from.

Fundamental guidelines for creating compelling and engaging visual content

It's one thing to create well-designed work. It's another to create content that compels the viewer to take action. To create such content, you have first to grab their attention.

The amount of visual content available and the amount of visual noise created by low-effort AI systems make it even harder to be seen these days.

To stand out, you need to focus on the two primary ways to get noticed: typography and imagery.

Both are equally important, but different audiences will be drawn to one or the other.

When it comes to typography, contrast is the most crucial part. The best typography is either very light color type on a dark background, or dark type on a light background. The type has to be clearly legible, even at small sizes. When there is a strong contrast between the type and the background, it's much easier to read.

Don't make your viewers work hard to consume your content. They'll move on to something easier to consume. You didn't make a new Marvel movie (sorry). People aren't clamoring for your latest marketing content. Make it legible and easy to read.

Think about the last billboard you saw. It probably had minimal, very large type. It also probably used high contrast to separate the copy from the background.

Figure 88: Midjourney prompt: a billboard by the side of a busy highway. The photo is being taken from the point of view of the driver; modified in Photoshop

There are times when you don't want high contrast. Products that are considered elegant or high-class will be more subtle. You'll see this on jewelry advertisements where the typography is thin, usually a little harder to read, and the colors don't jump off the page. When it comes to elegant design, subtlety is a good rule to follow.

Another way to grab attention is through imagery. The perfect photo can often do all the heavy lifting in your visual marketing. Sometimes, you want a photo where the person is looking directly at the viewer (through the camera). Other times, the photo will capture a moment that evokes the exact feeling you want to convey.

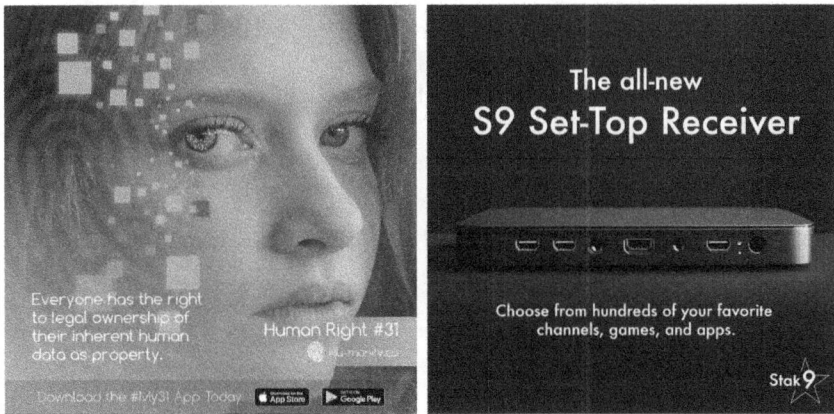

Figure 89: Ad from Hu-manity.co, Midjourney prompt: product photography, cable box; modified in Illustrator

Here are two Instagram images for different products. You can see how the first image draws you right in. You're almost challenged to look away. Her gaze captures you; then you look around and see the rest of the post. As I described in Chapter 2, faces are a great way to grab and hold attention.

The second ad is more of a classic product shot. The simplicity of the photo, background, and typography let you know that this is a product you should pay attention to. Because it is a dark product on a dark background, it portrays a feeling of elegance and a bit of mystery.

The goal is to create unique content that aligns with your other content. You must fight against your urge to create something new each time. I know it's hard. You were put on this planet to create new things, but it's better for the brand if you can be strategic with your creativity.

Maintaining brand consistency across all visuals

When working with creative people, their inclination is to be creative and make something new and exciting each time. As someone who understands the importance of brand consistency, it's your job to reign this in.

Nobody wants to be a robot and simply churn out content. AI systems can do that easier and cheaper than you can. Only a skilled human can create similar yet different content.

When Stan Lee was co-creating the modern Marvel Universe, he mastered the concept of "The illusion of change."[1] This was the act of telling stories that made you believe changes were happening. In retrospect, you realize there wasn't any actual change in the story. The hero is basically the same at the end of "her greatest battle" as before the battle started.

You must do the same with your visual content. Make it different but the same. It doesn't feel creatively rewarding, but consistency is important for the sake of the brand.

Your visual content needs to have common elements across each asset. This lets the viewer know they're all connected. Each asset is part of a larger story you're telling. As they go from one asset to another, it should be obvious that it's connected. Visuals are the easiest way to create this continuity.

Also, it saves time. If you can find a content type to templatize, do that. Data sheets or white papers should follow a template. For text-heavy documents and other items where design isn't going to make a big difference to the end user, create a template and churn those items out.*

Save your creative time, effort, and money for the assets where eye-catching visuals will make a demonstrable difference.

*(Obviously, you or the designer still need to make sure the copy flows well, keeping an eye on rivers, widows, hyphenation, image wraparounds, and more; but they don't have to exert the energy to design something from scratch each time.)

Creative storytelling techniques in visual marketing

Now that you know the rule of keeping your visuals on brand, you can learn how to break those rules.

When it's time for a new campaign, this is a time to add additional elements to your visuals. On top of the established visual brand identity, you can add new elements such as icons, lines, a new image treatment style, or maybe a different typeface. But don't do all of these things.

The core of your visuals needs to clearly be from your business. The additional elements can help the viewer realize when they're seeing something associated with the campaign. Because campaigns are temporary, you have the flexibility to add new elements.

If your brand is a straight line, campaigns allow you to bend the line five degrees or so. You're staying true to the visual brand, but you're just bending it a little for a short time.

Brand Variance
You can expand on your visual brand once it's been firmly established

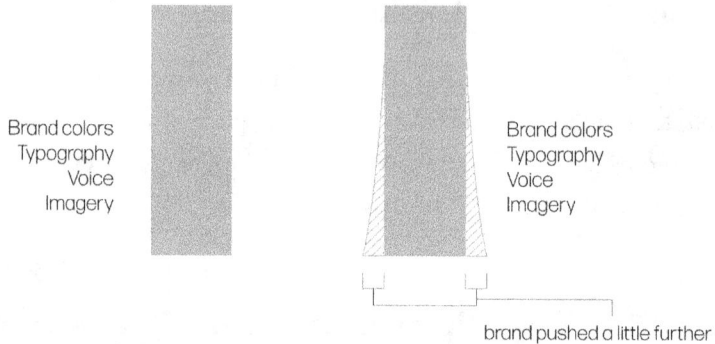

Brand colors
Typography
Voice
Imagery

Brand colors
Typography
Voice
Imagery

brand pushed a little further

Figure 90: Slight variations are allowed within brand guidelines

It will be tempting to adopt this as the new visual brand style because it feels new and fresh. But remember: you are not the audience. You look at your brand assets every day. You're probably bored of them. Your prospects aren't. They don't see—or think about—your visual brand nearly as much as you think they do. Keeping that consistency helps build your brand.

Some changes could be as simple as changing your headlines to all capital letters. Or maybe use a different weight for your official typeface. These little changes can help your content look a little different but still recognizable. Sometimes it can help to outsource the visuals for a campaign. Someone who doesn't work on the visual brand all day long can look at things with a fresh set of eyes.

The first time I was creative director for a tech company, we had an outside agency do some campaign work that included some branding elements. The agency's creative director, Courtney Smith Kramer, was able to do something new with the logo mark that I would never have thought of. I had been part of the development of this mark, yet she was able to modify it in a way that stayed true to the original while still adding a unique flair to the campaign.

Usually, I wouldn't approve of manipulating something as crucial as the brand mark, but it made sense for this particular use case. Courtney's fresh eyes allowed her to see potential that I was incapable of seeing because of my role as the protector of the brand.

Incorporating effective calls to action in visual content

"Design has to work, Art does not."

—*Donald Judd*

Most visual content is created to get the viewer to take an action. Sometimes, the calls-to-action (CTAs) are explicit. An email has one job and that's to get the viewer to click through and read more information on a website. The links are decorated in some way (underlined, a different color, or a button) to make it clear the viewer has to take an action to learn more.

Sometimes, the CTA is more implicit. An infographic gives the viewer information about their industry and, without being sales-y, the implicit CTA is that the viewer should read more from your business. You've already given the viewer valuable information, so it stands to reason that you have more information to help them with their goals.

A call to action is a great place to try A/B testing. Some phrases will res-onate better with your audience than others. Take the time to try different action phrases to encourage people to click (if it's a digital asset). Don't be afraid to try different button colors, shapes, or locations. There are some best practices that we covered in Chapter 3, but run your tests and deter-mine what works best for your audience.

This thinking can also be applied to copy or imagery. The two things to remember when it comes to A/B testing: only run one test at a time and make sure you're measuring your efforts. Otherwise, you're just doing extra work.

Optimization tips for visual content across different platforms

Just like using the right tool for the job, you must also use the right specs for the asset. Assets that could be printed, like a data sheet or white paper, should be output at 300 dpi (dots per inch). This is the normal measurement for printed materials.

For assets that will only live online, 72-150 pixels per inch (ppi) usually works. Static web graphics can be this lower resolution because 1) many screens have lower resolution and 2) it helps with load time. The larger the ppi, the larger the file size and the longer it takes to download from the web server. In the early computer days, 72 ppi was fine. But with the proliferation of high-resolution screens, ppi should be closer to 150-200 ppi now. This can slow down page load times, but in many cases, it's better than having a low-resolution, blurry image.

Simplified guide

- Print assets use dots-per-inch (dpi).
  - Ideal dpi for print: 300 dpi.
- Digital assets use pixels-per-inch (ppi).
  - Ideal ppi for digital: 72-150 ppi.

Digital images aren't measured in inches or millimeters, they're measured in pixels (px). Design programs will do these conversions, so you don't have to worry about this.

I'm sure you've been to a website where you had to sit and wait while the images were loaded. These images haven't been optimized for the web. It's highly unlikely that you'll need a 10" x 8" 300 ppi image on your website if the image is only going to be shown at 720px x 560px. Your image will be around ten times larger than it needs to be.

If you take that same 400px x 200px image at 72 ppi and increase it to 300 ppi, your file size is essentially jumping up to 1667px x 883px because images render at 72 ppi. You're increasing your file size and download time for almost zero benefit.

Figure 91: Photoshop Image Size window, 72 ppi

Figure 92: Photoshop Image Size window, 300 ppi, larger canvas size and file size

Here you can see what happens when you increase the same image from 72 pixels/inch to 300 pixels/inch. The file size jumps from 1.19 megabytes to 20.6 megabytes. I didn't change the width or height of the image. Photoshop automatically did this for me when I changed the resolution.

Figure 93: Photoshop Image Size window, 300 ppi, in inches, same canvas and file size

Ideally, your viewer sees the image size and resolution that works best on their device. Modern digital asset management (DAM) systems and content management systems (CMS) will be able to optimize images and feed the right size to the viewer based on their device settings.

If you are working on something that will be printed, it may be easier to adjust the units to inches. You can see that by changing the width and height to inches, it converts back to a system you're probably more familiar with. The file size has stayed the same because you didn't change the size of the image, just the way it's measured.

As we talked about in Chapter 10, you don't want to increase the size of a raster (pixel-based) image. It will distort the image and make it appear blurry or pixelated.

When you take a small image that is made up of pixels, the software has to estimate what it looks like when you add more pixels. This is called interpolation.[2] It happens whenever you change the pixel grid. Because it's an interpretation of what should happen between two pixels, the image loses fidelity when it increases (or decreases) in size.

For example, if you have a 10px x 10px image, you have 100 total pixels. Each pixel has a specific color assigned to it. If you were to expand that image to 1000px x 1000px, you now have 1,000,000 pixels. The software has to guess what goes in those new 999,900 pixels.

If you try to upsize a photo, suddenly, your perfectly round eyeballs become a series of gray squares in a circle-esque shape.

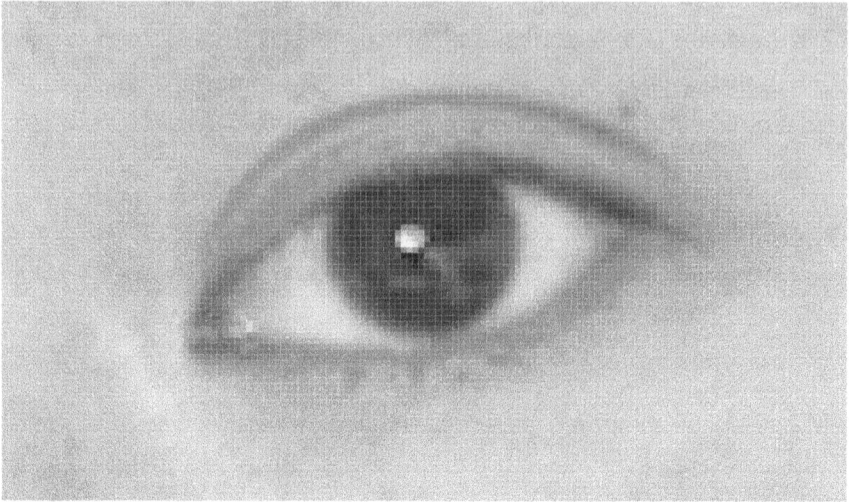

Figure 94: Flickr.com/Pascal Maramis, zoomed in to show individual pixels

There is no magic "enhance" button like you see on TV. But, thanks to AI, we are getting closer to this reality.

There are so many ways to create content. No two people do it the same. All that matters is that the end result does the job you want it to. Whether that is to build awareness, establish trust, or get the viewer to take an action, the content has a job. Quick reminder: "Looks cool" is not the job your content needs to do. It can look cool, but it has to do something else first.

When making your content, remember to keep it simple. Is what they are expected to do immediately apparent to the viewer? If not, keep working. Keep removing pieces until it's as simple as possible. Fight the inclination to put a lot in there. It's hard and counter-intuitive, but in the end you'll end up with more effective visual content.

Visual Cues

- It's one thing to create well-designed work. It's another to create content that compels the viewer to take action.

- To stand out from the noise, you need to focus on the two primary ways to get noticed: typography and imagery.
- Both are equally important, but different audiences will be drawn to one or the other.
- With typography, contrast (size, typeface, color, and more) is the most crucial part.
- Your visual content needs to have common elements across each asset.
- Push your visual brand forward, but not too far forward.
- You might get bored with your visual brand because you see it every day, but your prospects don't see it as frequently.

CHAPTER 13

Tools and Resources for Visual Marketers

"One machine can do the work of fifty ordinary [people]. No machine can do the work of one extraordinary [person]."

—*Elbert Hubbard*

When it comes to design tools, the most important thing to remember is that design skills are different from using the tools. Just having a microwave doesn't make you a chef. Having access to design tools doesn't make you a designer. Chapters 3 and 12 can help teach you the basics of design.

We covered many of the consumer-level design tools back in Chapter 10. Those tools are part of a wave of new design tools to help non-designers create visual content. They offer pre-built templates that can be customized to match your visual brand guidelines, including imagery, colors, and typography.

And then there are the pro-level tools. The barrier to entry is high. These tools require tens to hundreds of hours to be proficient. They are a remnant of a time when few people could be designers. These tools tend to be more expensive because their audience relies on them. These aren't weekend warriors trying to crop an image. These people use these tools all day, night, and weekend.

I've been using some of these tools for more than a quarter of a century (yikes), and there are many features I've never touched. These tools have become so robust that they can overwhelm new users. But for the pros, these tools empower them to produce creative work on a regular basis.

There are many tools that can be used for a myriad of use cases, but I'll touch on some of the more popular ones here.

Adobe Illustrator

Vector-based software that is ideal for logos, drawings, or other line-based imagery.

Illustrator dates back to the early days of Adobe, having begun development on the software in 1985. While it wasn't Adobe's original product, it helped the company expand its other products, specifically its electronic publishing language, PostScript.

Think of Illustrator as a way of drawing with a computer. But it's always 100% precise. You can reposition every point, change the curve on any line exactly as you want, or adjust the color or gradient of any element with absolute precision.

"Opening Adobe Illustrator for the first time can feel overwhelming, but the key is to focus on the basics and most important tools. Get comfortable with fundamental tools like the Pen, Shape, and Type tools—these are your building blocks. Keep your designs simple and scalable, use layers to organize your work, and always work with vector graphics to ensure scalability for any project. Start by creating color palettes and typography to build your brand's visual identity, and don't be afraid to explore Illustrator's pre-built templates for inspiration. Lastly, practice and patience are your greatest allies; the more you experiment, the more creative freedom you'll have when bringing your marketing ideas to life."

—Hollie Richmond, founder of Richmond Development Group.

216

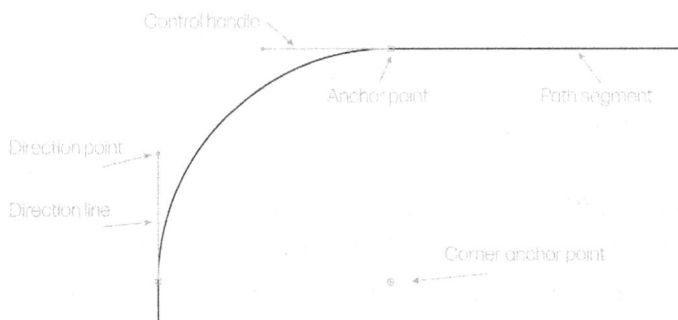

Figure 95: Parts of a vector line

Adobe Photoshop

Raster image editing tool. Manipulate pixels to anything you can imagine. From editing photos to creating never-before-seen dreamscapes, Photoshop gives you complete control over your visuals.

Photoshop became the company's flagship product when it was launched in 1989. The software is so popular that Photoshop is now a generic verb. Those of us of a certain age will remember when "Airbrush" was the common term for photo manipulation before Photoshop took the role of that verbal shorthand.

Photoshop has become a verb because it can do almost anything when it comes to image manipulation. With the introduction of generative AI features, Photoshop can create images just based on text prompts. This, combined with other tools within Photoshop, means that designers can create anything they can imagine.

Adobe InDesign

Desktop publishing tool. Ideal for page layouts and typography.

InDesign took over as the preeminent desktop publishing tool after Quark Xpress failed to update its software for the then-new Mac OS X. Adobe also started bundling Photoshop, Illustrator, and InDesign for the cost of Photoshop and Illustrator. InDesign was basically free because designers and creative teams were already paying for Photoshop and Illustrator. Before that, InDesign had replaced PageMaker as Adobe's primary desktop publishing application that was originally developed by Aldus.

InDesign works best for print-related projects. It is a layout tool for combining text and images. Though a lot of what InDesign does can be managed in Photoshop or Illustrator, InDesign is better when it comes to using typography. Leading, kerning, tracking, and all the other page layout type tricks are best performed in InDesign.

Adobe Premiere Pro

Video software ideal for cutting, arranging, and cleaning up footage.

The original version of the software, called Premiere, was one of the first desktop software applications for non-linear editing. This made it more affordable than buying a dedicated video editing system, like Avid. It's hard to remember a time when non-linear editing, the ability to edit something without having to restart from the beginning, was a novel idea.

Premiere Pro allows users to add clips to a timeline, add effects, transitions, and audio to create a full video. Premiere Pro also has many plugins which help to automate time-intensive tasks. From Premiere Pro, it's possible to export to many different video file types.

"The barrier to entry for marketing videos used to be incredibly steep and prohibitively expensive for anyone outside of an agency. But with the

advancement of pro-level computers, and editing suites evolving to sub-scription SaaS products, it's easier than ever to create captivating video. With this comes the double-edged sword of overload; the easier to learn and create, the easier to flood a market with video "just to have it." But what are you accomplishing? After someone watches your video, what do you want them to do next? A strong, succinct goal for your video strategy will help you rise above the sea of multimedia we swim in today.

In one of my first corporate video jobs, an interviewee asked me to "do my magic" to make her look into the camera instead of at her notes. At that time, there was no Adobe plugin for creating eye contact, but it was flattering that she thought I had the skills to do so. As AI technologies emerge and video production tools reach new heights, the possibilities may reach far beyond what we ever expected. However, I think I'll still recommend a retake—we can use a teleprompter this time."

—Laura Anthony, Multimedia Design Manager, EBSCO Information Services

Adobe After Effects

Video software made for motion graphics and visual effects.

After Effects is best used after a video has been produced and needs additional enhancements. Animation, special effects, and video compos-iting are all elements that can be added to a video with After Effects. Or, After Effects can be used to create animation without the need for previ-ously edited video. This type of animation is commonly known as motion graphics. If you wanted to add a lower-third graphic—a title at the bottom of a video that tells the viewer what they're watching—you would use After Effects for that.

*Figure 96: Midjourney prompt: a young black man wearing a
bucket hat. plain background; modified in Illustrator*

Final Cut Pro

Video editing software.

After leaving Adobe, Randy Ubillos and his team started developing software called KeyGrip for Macromedia (this was a few years before Adobe acquired Macromedia in 2005).[1] Before the newly renamed Macromedia Final Cut was released, the company decided to focus on web creation tools. Apple's Steve Jobs stepped in and acquired the development team and the code. Final Cut Pro was introduced as an Apple product in 1999.[2]

Final Cut Pro does a lot of what Adobe Premiere Pro does, but Final Cut Pro can be better suited for lighter, smaller projects. When it comes to choosing between the two, it comes down to preferences:

Do you want to pay a monthly subscription fee (Adobe Premiere Pro) or a one-time fee (Final Cut Pro)?

What is your computer operating system of choice? Since Final Cut Pro is an Apple product, you won't find it outside of the Mac ecosystem.

Do you need to share elements across different applications? If so, Adobe Premiere Pro might be better because it is part of the Adobe Creative Cloud suite of creative software tools.

Figma

User experience (UX) and user interface (UI) design tool built for collaboration.

Figma was released to the public in 2016 after four years of development. The founders, Dylan Field and Evan Wallace, were still in school and pivoted through different ideas during that time. Figma has become the pre-eminent UX and UI software with more than 40% of the collaborative design and prototyping market.[3] Just a few years ago, Sketch owned 71% of the market.[4] Figma knows how to work with designers to build a product they want to use. Adobe unsuccessfully tried to acquire Figma for $20 billion in 2022, much to the joy of the design community. Users were afraid Figma would end up as part of the Creative Cloud suite or other less-favorable business models.

As a cloud-based software, Figma allows designers to collaborate on the same files simultaneously. Designers can create layouts for web pages and product interfaces. Figma allows designers to build elements and reusable blocks that can be added to multiple pages without needing to recreate each section of a page.

The atomic design system:[5]

The Atomic Design System

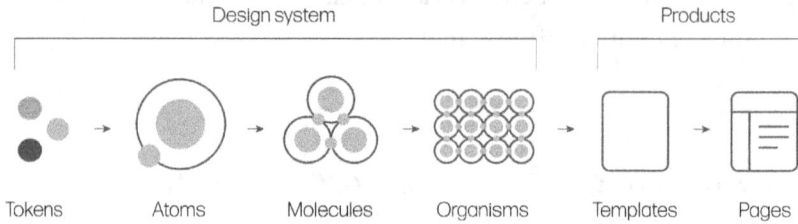

Design system   Products

Tokens   Atoms   Molecules   Organisms   Templates   Pages

Figure 97: Atomic design system

Creating a system like this allows users to change a piece—let's use a molecule in this instance—and have that change reflected everywhere that molecule is used across the document.

These systems take a while to build out, but once they're in place, they streamline the entire process. If you were to change your primary brand color from red to purple, you could update that in one place, and it would automatically update across all your pages or screens.

Recommendations for resources, blogs, and books for further learning

Before jumping into design tools, I highly recommend learning the basics of design. For me, the most important things to learn in design are setting up a visual hierarchy and creating a path for the user's eye to flow around your asset. How people visually consume information changes between print and digital, but many of the basics are still the same. HubSpot's blog is a great source of design information for marketers who are looking to up their game. They even have an article on the topic of visual hierarchy at: https://blog.hubspot.com/marketing/visual-hierarchy

The content with the most contrast will get noticed first. Vary your type sizes so readers know in which order they should consume content. If you want a deep dive on typography, I recommend Robert Bringhurst's *The Elements of Typographic Style*. It has far more information than any non-designer would need to know, but it also has the basics that will make you realize why you don't create marketing content that looks like the essays you wrote in school.

If you're looking for design inspiration, Dribbble.com (yes, it has three b's in the domain name) can be a good source. However, be careful not to become too enamored with the designs posted there. Many of the designs posted there were not created for real-world use cases. These are "cool" designs that are closer to art than design.

Remember, design has a job to do. It's the design's job to get the viewer to take an action. Art can have that impact, but it's not the primary reason for art.

YouTube is a great resource for learning about design. Once you've figured out visual hierarchy and user eye flow, work on spacing. As I mentioned before, when looking at design portfolios, the first thing I notice is spacing and alignment. There is an underlying, invisible grid to every good design. This page has a grid. There is a science to layout and if you can learn the basics, it gives your visual content a step up.

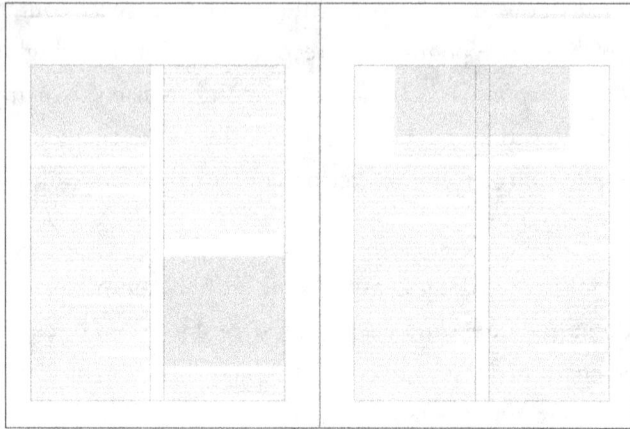

Figure 98: Example of the underlying grid of a page

Tips for staying updated with the latest tools and technologies: Communities

These days, with the rapid proliferation of AI across every digital discipline, it can be hard to stay on top of all the changes. For this, I highly recommend finding a community or three that is comprised of people who are digging into the "next big thing."

These communities can be found in Discord, Slack, social media, or the real world.

Listen to podcasts with people who are pushing boundaries. Podcasts can be better than just a written bio or interview because podcasts can get deeper and allow the guest to discuss how they stay up to date.

Subscribe to newsletters that discuss design trends. Some will detail successful designs and, most importantly, why they work. As you learn the difference between successful and unsuccessful design, it can help to have someone explain why some visual content performs better than others.

Forward-thinking companies will also have a community dedicated to the audience who want to learn more. Adobe has multiple Discord channels. Figma has an online community.

I am part of a few communities, and I learn so much from them. I recommend trying a paid community. These are the people who are willing to spend the time and effort to work together, try new things, and push the boundaries of marketing. And if you're spending money on it, you're more likely to force yourself to participate.

You need to get outside of your four walls to see what else is going on out in the world. If you aren't able to attend in-person events, online communities are the next best thing. I'm a part of one community, Mark Schaefer's RISE community, that has an active Discord server. We chat about an array of topics related to marketing. But we also have near-weekly Zoom get-togethers where industry experts come in, and we discuss their areas of expertise. It's infinitely better than a webinar where a faceless voice speaks over slides in a one-way conversation.

If you're looking for groups that are more focused on the design side of things, social media can also be a good place to find communities. There are groups like Designers Talk on LinkedIn and the Design Threads hashtag on Threads or Bluesky where you can be introduced to people trying new things and talking about the industry.

My suggestion for finding success in any group is to help first. See how you can contribute to the group before finding ways to extract value. If you go in there trying to find work or looking for someone to help with your project, you won't find many takers.

Integrating multiple tools for a streamlined workflow

One of the nice things about using a suite of products, like Adobe Creative Cloud, is elements like shared libraries.

When you create a library with your logo, colors, or other design elements, you can then use those elements in Photoshop, Premiere Pro, or any other Adobe Creative Cloud application. This means that when you add a vector logo to your new library in Illustrator, you can then pull that logo into a Photoshop file. Then, if you want to change the logo's color, you can update it in Illustrator. That logo will be automatically updated in Photoshop or anywhere else you've added the logo from your library. Like Figma elements, an Adobe library can save you so much time. It will also help reduce mistakes caused by forgetting to update something in a different file.

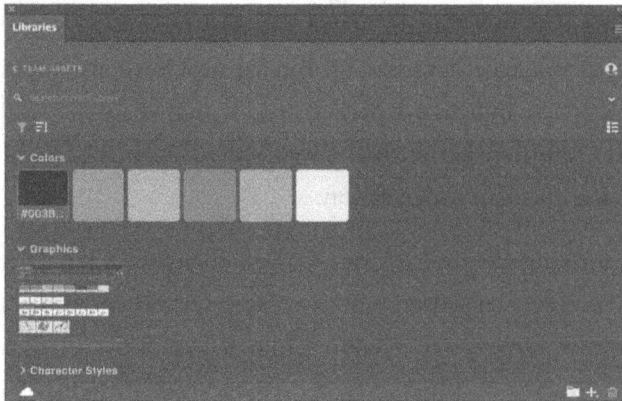

Figure 99: Adobe Libraries that can be shared across applications and teams

"My creative department has 11 designers across three teams who design material for hundreds of different products that span six different industries. There is also the added challenge of designing for a global audience, as we must tailor our materials for diverse cultural preferences and market needs across dozens of countries. It is vital that we maintain brand integrity while accommodating the unique needs of each audience.

To achieve this, we have adopted the use of Adobe Creative Cloud Libraries. We have separate libraries for brand assets that all designers have access to. Pulling assets from the same libraries encourages designers to have creative freedom while staying within the brand guidelines and supporting alignment. For optimized searching, we gave each asset detailed names such as 'book library read' for a 'book' icon. This saves the designers time, allowing them to easily search for an icon directly from their Adobe programs, sparing them from manually browsing a large document of icons. Using Creative Cloud Libraries has enhanced the consistency of design assets, leading to a stronger and more cohesive brand identity.

—Megan Behrendt, Director of Marketing Design and UX, EBSCO Information Services

You'll want to start integrating generative AI tools with your other design tools. This isn't going away, so it makes sense to start practicing now. Learning what tool is best at different tasks can make your life much easier. As I mentioned in the Adobe InDesign section, many tools can do similar tasks, but some are better than others.

Let's try a quick exercise: open a vector logo in Adobe Illustrator and make it all white. Then, create an image in Midjourney. Add that image to Adobe Photoshop. If it's not quite what you want, you can do a little Firefly editing to remove an object or add space to change the image's dimensions. Then drag in your logo as a smart object. From here, you can add additional Photoshop effects to the logo or make the logo semi-transparent. Once you're good with that, you can create a new Adobe InDesign file and import the image. Feel free to flow text around that image, and voila! You have now used four different applications to create a flyer or an advertisement. (Okay, that exercise isn't quick, but you can start seeing how these tools work together.)

Reporting tools for visual marketing success

It's one thing to create great visual content. And even better to measure its performance. If you're not the business owner, you also need to show how this work positively impacts the bottom line.

You need to synthesize the data into an executive overview. Most executives don't have time to comb through your spreadsheets filled with an array of metrics. You and I know that many of these metrics aren't necessarily vanity metrics, but an executive doesn't have time to see how many likes a particular social post received.

Executives want to know how the work you're doing is helping the company make more money. Full stop.

Your job now is to create an easy way for the executive to consume the data to see the return on investment (ROI). If you have an exec who trusts you, you might want to set up a live dashboard that allows her to see updated statistics whenever she wants. If there isn't trust, then you could have an executive who starts making declarations about your visual content before it has had a chance to properly perform. In this scenario, a live dashboard would be a bad idea.

For those with a trusting boss(es), there are tools like Tableau, Looker Studio, Power BI, or other data dashboard tools that, when properly integrated into marketing automation and customer-relationship management tools, will show how assets are performing.

Just imagine how great it would be if you got a message from an executive saying, "I see the most recent white paper has led to $400,000 in new pipeline!" Or if they ask, "Why isn't our ad campaign performing better?" you can open the dashboard to show that the campaign just started this past Thursday, so it's still getting optimized.

Reporting on your visual marketing activities will help build trust. Showing how marketing is helping the company will build that trust and open up more opportunities in the future.

Most executives want to know how to spend a dollar to get five dollars back. We all know marketing is a great way to do that. Showing positive results is the best way to get that initial dollar freed up so you can do the creative work.

And speaking of ways to get your creative spend to go a little further …

Visual Cues

- The barrier to entry is high on pro-level design software.
- Design software and design skills are two different skill sets.
- Learning the basics of design first will help when you're using the software.
- Art and design are two separate things. Design has a job to do (get the viewer to take an action).
- Join online communities to help you stay current with design trends.
- Knowing the tools will empower you to use the right tool at the right time for the right task.
- Set up reports to show the ROI of your visual marketing efforts.

CHAPTER 14:

Enhancing Visual Marketing with AI

"By far, the greatest danger of Artificial Intelligence is that people conclude too early that they understand it."

—*Eliezer Yudkowsky*

Text-to-image applications started to gain attention in mid-2022. A few people tried them out, but they were mostly ignored because they weren't that great. I know I initially dismissed the idea when I heard about it. I thought a computer system couldn't replicate what designers and other creatives do.

But on November 30, 2022, ChatGPT was released, opening the floodgates of generative AI. Even though ChatGPT was focused on generating words, this introduced many new people to the idea of using generative AI for content and image creation. Suddenly, "How can we use AI in our marketing?" became the most popular question in conference rooms and Zoom meetings worldwide.

Once AI became a hot topic in the consumer space, many companies jumped in to promote their AI capabilities. AI was a differentiator, even if many of these companies had tools that were already using AI behind the scenes. The promotion of AI capabilities far outpaced the actual capabilities of AI.

Before we get too deep, let's break down a few terms you may need to know.

Artificial Intelligence (AI)

The ability of machines to perform tasks that normally require human intelligence, such as recognizing images, understanding language, and making decisions.

Machine Learning (ML)

A subset of AI where systems improve their performance based on data without explicit programming. It learns from patterns.

Large-Language Models (LLMs)

A type of AI designed to understand and generate human language. These models are trained on massive amounts of text data, enabling them to create responses to various prompts (questions or commands).

Generative AI

AI that creates new content based on patterns it has learned from existing data.

You may not need this information today or tomorrow, but it's good to know the difference. If you're just getting started with generative AI, focus on small experiments first. It could be too much if you try to do everything at the start.

The role of AI in automating visual content creation and personalization

Generative AI can help with many tasks required in visual content creation. One area where generative AI can save a lot of time is social media.

Due to different social platforms using different image sizes, AI can create social images in various aspect ratios. Adobe Photoshop's generative fill tool allows you to extend pictures without using the Clone tool to fill in empty space. The results are significantly better, and much easier to use.

You could also use generative AI to help personalize your visual content. If you have an image you want to use for a campaign, you could run it through a system like Midjourney or Adobe Photoshop to swap out the person in the image. This allows you to create images with people who look like they belong to that geographic region. The thinking behind this is that you may not want to use a red-haired, freckled woman on a campaign in Japan.

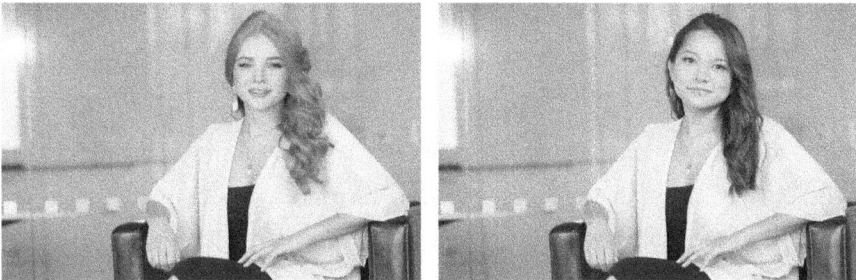

Figure 100: Pexels.com/divinetechygirl; modified in Photoshop

Netflix famously monitors what you consume so it can offer additional programming that will likely appeal to you. Did you know that it does this with thumbnails too?

Netflix uses a process called Aesthetic Visual Analysis (AVA) to determine which personalized thumbnails it should show you. Netflix uses a set of algorithms to go through the content and pick the best potential thumbnails. It creates metadata for every single frame! This allows the streaming giant to show you thumbnails that are most likely to appeal to you.[1]

For example, if you just watched *The Blindside* with Sandra Bullock, the thumbnail for *Speed* might show her rather than Keanu Reeves. Your thumbnails could change from day to day based on what you've recently viewed, as well as the viewing history of other people who have been identified to be similar to you.

Examples of AI-driven tools and platforms* for visual marketing

This section needs to come with a very large asterisk. The AI landscape is changing so quickly that things could have completely changed from when I wrote this to when it was published and when you got to this chapter. And they probably have. But let's talk about a few industry leaders that generate visual content.

Midjourney was one of the early front runners in the generative AI image game. Initially, users had to access the Discord messaging platform to use Midjourney, which created a barrier to entry. In mid-2024, Midjourney came to the web, and now anyone can access the platform without having to figure out how to use Discord.

Midjourney allows you to type a prompt and it generates four options. From there, you can create variations of one of the images. Or, if you're happy with one of the options, you can upsize the image and save it.

If you want to get granular, there are a handful of adjustments you can make before you create your initial images.

Figure 101: Midjourney settings menu

DALL-E is OpenAI's version of an AI image generator. It was initially released before OpenAI released its flagship product, ChatGPT. Now, DALL-E is included with a ChatGPT subscription. There are a couple of differences between Midjourney and DALL-E. Quick fact: DALL-E gets its name from artist Salvador Dalí and the Pixar robot WALL-E.

The biggest difference is you can have a back-and-forth conversation with DALL-E. Because it is part of ChatGPT, you can use nuance to iterate an image. Midjourney is more of a call-and-response interaction. If you're trying to iterate in Midjourney, use the Variation function or write a new prompt with the differences you want to be included. Both systems can sometimes get stuck in a rut and continue to output elements of the image you don't want. You might have to use a new channel to clear out some visual aspects you can't shake.

For example, if you requested an elderly man at one point, it could continue to create images with elderly men even if you've changed that part of the prompt.

The other big difference between DALL-E and Midjourney is the ability to edit parts of an image in DALL-E. Once you have created an image, you can use a brush effect to highlight areas you want changed and then tell DALL-E what to put in that place.

For example, if you create an image of a young girl playing with a cat, you can highlight the cat and replace it with a dog

Figure 102: Dall-E prompt: "A young girl playing with a cat." Then, "Please make this a small dog"

Meta AI is the generative AI tool from the makers of Instagram and Facebook.

Meta AI is free for people who have a Facebook account. Like other systems, it allows you to type in a prompt and it spits out an image. Unlike other offerings, these images come watermarked. There is also a feature to do some minor animation that outputs as an MP4 file.

For those worried about AI LLMs (large language models) that are created using stolen imagery, Adobe Firefly has only been trained on Adobe-licensed images. Adobe also has a compensation system for contributors.[2]

The service is free, but you need to create an account to access the results of your prompt.

Adobe Firefly is also the generative AI engine used in Adobe Photoshop and Adobe Illustrator.

Sora is OpenAI's answer to generative AI for video. By typing a simple prompt, an incredible video can be created. It can be used as b-roll or backgrounds for other information.

The impact of AI on content optimization and audience targeting

AI's impact on all marketing will be substantial. In the early days of generative AI, it looked like a bad toupee. Everyone knew the image and copy weren't real and that those companies were covering for deficiencies, either in budget or skill. As AI-generated content improves, it will be harder to tell what is real and what is AI-produced.

AI is great at crunching data and letting you see the information that will be most helpful. You can use AI to comb through the analytics of your content to see what is performing well and what isn't. If you have a marketing automation system and customer relationship management (CRM) platform, you should be able to identify who is consuming your content. Pulling this data into an AI platform (make sure not to share any personal identifiable information [PII] or confidential information) will show you which audiences are consuming certain types of content.

Once the data is in the system, you can ask more questions to get better insights into your viewers and their habits. Many SaaS tools now have AI capabilities built into the software, so you don't have to worry about adding this information to ChatGPT, Looker Studio (formerly Google Data Studio), Airtable, or another system.

AI can also help you with audience segmentation. You can identify different segments based on behavior, preference, or demographics that you may not have noticed before. You can then measure the actions that segment takes with Google Analytics 4 or a marketing automation platform.

Advanced digital systems can also leverage AI to serve more information to viewers based on the content they are consuming. It takes a while to set up, but once you connect all the dots of your content, let AI automatically deliver the right content to the right audience.

You see this on Amazon. Whenever you look at an item, there are always suggestions for similar products or products usually purchased by people who purchase the product you're viewing. This is one of the world's largest companies using AI to create a tailored experience just for you. Every time you click on something, Amazon learns a little more about you. It does this because the better it knows you, the better it can sell you the things you need or want.

The beauty of AI is automating tasks so you can focus on other tasks. For a company of Amazon's size, it would be impossible to manually personalize experiences, so it invested in the infrastructure to enable personalization at scale.

Ethical considerations and challenges in using AI for visual marketing

I alluded to this earlier, but there are ethical concerns when using AI-generated visual or written content. Because we don't know what makes up these large language models (LLMs), it's impossible to know what went into the training of these tools. Sometimes you'll hear the term "black box" when people refer to LLMs because we can't see what's in there.

This means it's entirely possible (and highly likely) that these models were trained on copyrighted material. Many of these companies allegedly illegally scraped and ingested content owned by someone else.

When you type a prompt into a generative AI tool, it could create something based on stolen property. Somebody owned the rights to the original content. The AI companies allegedly potentially stole that content, which is the foundation for the newly created content that you requested from the generative AI system.

How would you feel if you found out companies were profiting from your hard work? And then the people buying that stolen content are turning around and profiting themselves? It wouldn't feel good if everyone was making money based on your work except for you.

This is where the ethical questions around AI must be considered.

Adobe has taken the step to only train its LLM on content it has licensed. I don't know what this means in the long run for people who licensed their content to Adobe, but it's better than what everyone else is doing.

Meta admitted using publicly available images and content on its platforms like Facebook and Instagram.

"We don't train on private stuff, we don't train on stuff that people share with their friends, we do train on things that are public."

—Chris Cox, Meta Chief Product Officer[3]

This means that when you publicly post an image of your pets, your kids, or your rambunctious Saturday night, Meta uses that information to train its LLM. Many people are not comfortable with this idea. But even more aren't aware that Meta relies on its billions of users to train its LLM.

There are two sides of this equation that you have to consider: What type of data are you using with your generative AI work? And do you know if your data is being used to train LLMs?

Future possibilities for AI in visual content strategy

Generative AI continues to improve with each new release. As Paul Roetzer of the Marketing AI Institute says, "The AI you are using [today] is the worst and least capable AI you will ever use."

It's only getting better. And it's getting better quickly.

That's good news if you plan on using AI in your everyday visual marketing work. But it's bad news if you're not using it. Before you know it, the imagery and copy that is being generated will look like professionals created it.

You can ask ChatGPT to create a visual content strategy for you. Then you can take the appropriate actions to create the necessary assets and distribute them.

In the (very near) future, you could ask a system like Jasper to create a visual content strategy ... and deliverables ... and distribute them when and where you want them published.

Right now, we still need a human to review the content. But before you know it, more and more of this will be automated.

Is it the right thing to do? That's for you to determine.

Is your business likely to adopt generative AI? If so, it's time you learn how to use it and position yourself as the expert in this space. Don't get left behind.

Case studies of brands successfully leveraging AI in their visual marketing

The respected newspaper The Economist needed to shake things up when it noticed its readership dropping in 2017. It relied on AI to enhance its programmatic advertising strategy.

It captured user data and used AI to identify a segment of its potential audience that wouldn't normally buy a subscription to a publication like The Economist. It then served up ads targeted specifically to its prospective audience.

The more it learned about these potential readers and created lookalike audiences (people who share certain characteristics with the audience you have already identified), the better it could tailor its visual marketing. And it paid off: The Economist garnered 3.6 million new readers. This led to a 10:1 return on investment (ROI).[4]

One aspect that led to the success of The Economist's campaigns was the use of near real-time content creation to run ads. If generative AI had been available at the time, the historic publisher could have run multiple variations even faster.

Beauty juggernaut L'Oréal relies on its in-house Generative AI Task Force and GenAI Content Lab to structure its AI use. The task force helps establish and enforce responsible AI use. For a company of L'Oréal's size, it's great to see it establishing AI guardrails during the formative time of AI integration.

Due to the fact that nobody knows the source of generative AI imagery, L'Oréal doesn't use facial images generated by AI in any of its marketing. The same applies to images of skin, body, or hair. This makes sense for a company that needs to be authentic when promoting products that enhance these body parts.

L'Oreal uses generative AI for brainstorming ideas and extending photo-shoots. The technology enhances the company's existing work and creates flexibility to showcase its products.

> *"We believe that technology can push the boundaries of what is possible. We can cater to the infinite diversity of beauty needs, and therefore, we are also empowering our consumers with elevated beauty services."*
>
> —*Asmita Dubey, L'Oréal chief digital and marketing officer*[5]

Humanity's role in AI

Generative AI is having a significant impact on visual marketing. Being able to automate parts of the creative process will allow companies and marketers to move faster and operate at a larger scale. For those marketers who are data-driven, generative AI will allow you to try different options and then easily analyze the data to determine how to run future visual marketing campaigns.

We're still in the early days of AI and generative AI. The methodologies you adopt today will probably differ in a year or two. However, learning how to use this powerful new weapon will allow you to build your capabilities for the future.

AI is here to augment creativity, not replace it. Relying too much on AI-generated content will damage your brand's overall reputation because it is unoriginal and reveals companies that take shortcuts and cut costs. Many companies will use AI-generated content in their visual marketing and it will be noticeable...in a bad way. Even if the output is cool, you don't want your brand associated with these negative traits.

These systems still need human oversight. Sometimes, these systems get it wrong. If you think of them as interns, you know that you have to monitor what an intern does until they figure out how to do their jobs. It's the same with an AI system.

Human creativity will always be more organic than AI-generated content. The reason there is such a huge organic grocery market is that people still crave natural things. Artificial may be cheaper and faster to produce, but that doesn't mean everyone wants it.

As Robert Rose says, "Some amount of friction in learning how to do the thing is an important part of the human condition."[6] We're built to create stuff. Learning how to create can be painful. Yes, it's easier to whip up something in a generative AI system than to take the time to learn how to create it by hand. However, there is a level of pride and accomplishment that is missing when it comes to AI-generated content.

Visual Cues

- Everyone is trying to figure out how to incorporate AI into their workflows.
- Don't worry, most teams are still very early in this process.
- AI is being baked into most software to enhance your productivity.
- Use generative AI to translate and localize your content (make sure to double-check it).
- AI is getting better every day. Don't dismiss it because you tried it once and it created an image with a six-fingered hand.
- There are ethical considerations when using generative AI.
- Humans are made to build stuff.
- Don't outsource your creative thinking.

CHAPTER 15

Visual Marketing Trends and Future Directions

"You can't use up creativity. The more you use, the more you have."

—*Maya Angelou*

Forecasting the future within marketing can be a dangerous game. None of us know when trends will change or when the major tech companies will change an algorithm and all our current digital marketing tactics will stop working.

The good news is that the future is based on the past. The basics of marketing and communicating with prospects and customers remain consistent. What we're communicating hasn't changed, but the way in which we communicate is in a constant state of flux.

Analysis of current and emerging trends in visual marketing

Visuals aren't new. Neither is marketing. And visual marketing isn't new, either. Just like anything with a long lineage, some things change, some things stay the same. The basics of visual marketing remain: Engage the audience, convey an emotion so it grabs real estate in the viewer's mind, and then get them to take an action (if that is the goal).

Beyond that, trends are constantly changing.

Many of the changes we see these days are due to technology. There is still a generation of visual marketers who were doing this before the Internet was a thing. Back then, TV ads, billboards, newspapers, and magazines were the best visual marketing methods.

These days, you can place visual marketing almost everywhere. Screens surround our lives. And as technology progresses, they won't even be restricted to screens. You'll be able to run marketing campaigns anywhere.

Some of the trends we see today are vertical video. YouTube Shorts, Instagram Reels, and other vertical video platforms drive a ton of engagement. In 2023, 60% of marketers rethought their visual content strategy to focus more on vertical video. These short but engaging videos appeal to a growing audience.[1]

AI-produced content will continue to infiltrate visual marketing. As the technology improves, the visuals and copy that AI produces will be more human-like. The influx of AI-generated content will lead to the next revolution in visual marketing.

As far as visual trends, if you want to experiment with trends, you can use campaigns to test-drive the latest eye-catching techniques. In the late 2010s and early 2020s, many cutting-edge businesses used pinks and purples on dark backgrounds in their visual marketing work. Because campaigns only run for a limited time, you can adopt some of these trends if they fit within the boundaries of your existing visual brand standards.

You should never build your visual brand around a trend because trends change. The time and effort required to build a visual brand means you should not change it every 18–24 months. A trend-based visual brand signifies to the audience that your business is temporary.

Soft drinks aimed at younger audiences often use trendy visuals because it is the easiest way to grab their attention. Brands like Mountain Dew and

Sprite always keep the core elements of their visual identities intact even when they adopt trendy visuals.[2]

Figure 103: Mountain Dew's visual identity evolution

Predictions for the future of visual marketing strategies and technologies

A reaction to the flood of AI-generated content will lead to the pendulum swinging back toward organic, artisanal marketing. We're already starting to see this at some levels. Teens have begun referring to AI-generated art as "Boomer art." And we all know that for this group, the biggest insult is to call something old. After the millennials and Gen Z spent the last decade or two insulting the baby boomer generation, Gen Alpha is following in their footsteps.

(I'm Gen X, so I get to sit back and watch. But I digress.)

You'll start to see a return to in-person events and print marketing. After staring at screens for years, people are hungry for real human experiences. In-person events allow attendees to have person-to-person conversations you can't get with a webinar or virtual roundtable. There is nothing like commiserating with someone in a similar situation at a different company and then working toward a solution.

Print marketing allows you to stand out because so few businesses do it. It's expensive, and proofing takes longer because, unlike digital, there are no more edits once it's printed. It's also harder to measure than digital.

As companies have abandoned print, there is an opportunity to stand out. The least crowded inbox is the one at the end of your driveway. Print can't be ignored by simply clicking and deleting it. It's a tangible thing held in your hands and glanced at. If it's visually appealing, people will take the time to flip through it.

As technology like generative AI improves, we'll see more personalization. Being able to easily translate your content into different languages or swap out images to better reflect the local audience will make your content more effective. In addition to translation, technology will also allow you to localize your content.

The role of emerging technologies (VR, AR, 3D imaging) in visual marketing

We're in an interesting place on the extended reality (XR) hype cycle. In the early 2020s, there was a lot of hype around the metaverse. It came on the heels of the crypto and non-fungible token (NFT) boom. A lot of this hype resulted from people being stuck at home during the COVID-19 pandemic.

Once the hype died down and the general public walked away from fad-chasing apps that were trying to cash in on the buzzy new technology, serious businesses could focus on building useful applications.

Extended reality environments offer a new world for visual marketing.

Virtual reality (VR) hit another inflection point in 2024. When Apple introduced the Apple Vision Pro, it created a device that lets people consume content in a fully immersive environment. The Apple Vision Pro was also built for work, unlike previous VR devices. While the technology looks impressive, it hasn't been adopted at the rate VR aficionados hoped for.

Though the audience is small, this could be an opportunity if you sell products to early adopters with a lot of disposable income. Building an application or working with partners to add your messaging to their applications would help get your marketing efforts in front of a potentially lucrative audience.

For augmented reality (AR), adding visual marketing elements to a scene people are already experiencing is possible. Imagine a woman using an AR app on her smartphone to view something and, suddenly, your imagery appears off to the side. In some ways, it could perfectly blend into the environment, or it could visually scream out for attention. Many variables go into something like this, but the opportunities are limitless because it's a brand-new area that hasn't been fully developed yet.

AR has proven very good at training for hands-on roles. For people who have to repair complex machinery, using an AR headset will allow them to see the steps they have to follow to fix something. For complex machinery that moves around, such as helicopters or submarines, it can be much easier to use AR to train someone local to inspect an engine than to have full-time mechanics travel with the machinery.

Companies that offer this technology could help subsidize the price by offering in-app advertising at the right times. I don't want the person inspecting my next flight to be distracted by a Disney ad, but there could be opportunities to do visual marketing.

While VR or AR haven't been widely adopted, some businesses are working to create mixed reality experiences. Mobeus, a startup based in

New Jersey, is working with some top consumer and business brands to build virtual environments for consumers to have metaverse-like experiences without the awkward hardware. Just by using a regular laptop, people can have an experience similar to walking into a store and interacting with a sales representative. A huge audience of prospects still want to have a conversation before making a purchase.

Preparing your marketing strategy for future visual trends

Knowing that your audiences won't always be limited by phone, computer, and TV screens means you need to look for new opportunities. Just think; at some point, someone had the idea to run video ads on the gas pump. That was a novel idea, but someone realized a captive audience existed. And where there's an audience, there's money to be made.

Currently, most visual marketing takes place on screens of various sizes and locations. But don't forget about analog visual marketing. Billboards, print publications, apparel, or other forms of printed materials offer different ways to reach audiences.

The secret is being prepared for when a new marketing avenue arrives. If you've followed the advice throughout this book, you've established ways to scale your visual marketing efforts to accommodate additional platforms.

For something like The Sphere in Las Vegas, businesses are adapting their work to fit a giant round screen. Most creative teams haven't had to think in these dimensions before. The video is displayed in 16k resolution and has to be cut into slices to fill the space.[3] The file sizes for displays like this are enormous, so make sure you have computers powerful enough to render animations at 2608 x 2304 pixels and 60fps (frames per second).

Figure 104: iStock.com/Suzyanne16

One challenge with new technology is a lack of designers who can handle brand-new environments. If you find yourself exploring new lands, reach out to the venue to see if they recommend anyone. Otherwise, you can look around Instagram or Reddit to find potential partners doing this cutting-edge work.

If you find yourself working with an agency or partner pitching outside-the-box ideas, stay in contact with them. Even if you don't go with their ideas right now, those are the types of partners who can advise you when you're ready to try something new. Early adopters can save your skin when something new comes up because these projects always seem to have the shortest timeline.

The importance of adaptability and continuous learning in marketing

As content marketing leader Robert Rose says,

"Marketing is the combination of art and science. If it were just science, we'd have figured it out by now."

Marketing is always changing. How people consume our messages, the platforms upon which we market, budgets, technology, and a myriad of other influences force us to be in a constant state of adaptation.

This can be frustrating or scary for people. Just because something worked yesterday doesn't mean it will work tomorrow. SEO is a great example of this. Google is constantly tweaking its algorithm to prevent SEO experts from gaming the system. Its goal is to serve up more advertising before finding the information you want to see.

No matter how good you are, you must be wary of getting passed by. There will always be someone younger, cheaper, and more in tune with modern trends than you. You must stay on top of modern advances. What you offer is the ability to take your years of experience and combine them with the latest trends in marketing.

Experience + adaptability = success when it comes to marketing.

Now, this doesn't mean you should chase every trend. You have to utilize the proper fashion for your unique audience. Chasing trends leads to a lot of burned time, effort, and money. There can be benefits to being early to a new marketing methodology–early bloggers saw success if they stuck with it–but for every new trend that stuck around, there are dozens that never made it past a few months. How much time have you spent on Clubhouse's audio-only platform in the past few weeks? Leave a comment on my MySpace page and let me know. ;)

I think it's important to at least sign up for each new buzzy app. You can spend 10-15 minutes to see if it makes sense for you. And more importantly, it allows you to protect your username in case the platform takes off. TikTok hasn't made sense as a platform for me to focus on, but I registered my username back when it was called Musical.ly. I had no interest in making Gen Z-focused lip-sync videos on Musical.ly, but I grabbed my @JimMacLeod handle. Then when it was merged into TikTok in 2018, I already had my username secured. When/if it makes sense for me to start using TikTok, I'll be ready to expand my brand further because I have the same username I use across many different platforms.

Bottom line: Pay attention to trends. Be willing to try them out for a few minutes. Be willing to ditch them if they don't make sense for your audience.

Encouraging innovation and experimentation in visual marketing

Trying new things not only energizes your creative side; it can also help engage your audience. You never know where a new idea will come from. Consume a lot of new experiences. Keep collecting inputs and let your brain blend those together so the next time you're working on creative work, something new will appear magically.

In *The Creative Curve*, Allen Gannett talks about the myth of creativity. "It turns out that the mythology around creativity is just that, myth. You do not have to be born with some X-Men-like super-power to achieve great artist or entrepreneurial heights." Creativity isn't a gift people are born with; it isn't something that arrives via divine intervention. Creativity is like a muscle; the more you use it, the better it gets.

Knowing this, you can get started with your visual marketing efforts. Create something new, something that is exciting for you. More likely than not, you are not the audience, but if it's exciting to you, think about how your audience may react.

When I first started as a designer, I just wanted to make cool visuals. Then I learned that I needed to make effective visuals. The pre-determined audience is the group that has to be engaged by the visuals so they take the action you want them to take.

If that audience gets bored with what you're producing, it's time to change it up. My view has been that once a visual identity has been created and well established (this usually takes two to three years), you can start to extend the visual brand. This allows you to take your visual marketing into newer areas.

I'm not saying you should introduce a complementary color outside of your brand colors, but you could shift the established colors just a little. You could apply a different filter to your photography. Or maybe introduce a playful typeface as a secondary expressive typeface to accompany your corporate sans-serif typeface.

Be willing to try new things by stretching what you have already done. Take it a step further. The viewer should know that what they see is from you, but it's new. Since you've already established a strong visual marketing identity, pushing it a few degrees past your current state should be easy and fun.

Chasing trends can be a distraction to your long-term visual brand-building work. Instead, think about how you can have a considered, slow evolution of your visual marketing. This will signal to the market that your business is ever moving forward.

Jumping from trend to trend takes a lot of time and energy. Focus on building your visual brand identity. From here, you can try minor experiments with your visual marketing. This can be hard for creative people who want to make something new and exciting each time, but it will help your business in the long run.

Visual Cues

- The continual state of change in technology can seem overwhelming to keep up with.

- The basics of marketing haven't changed.

- How we do marketing is in a constant state of flux.

- The basics of visual marketing remain: Engage the audience, convey an emotion so it grabs real estate in the viewer's mind, and then get them to take an action.

- Print is an opportunity to stand out since most businesses abandoned it.

- Extended reality (XR) will play a role in the future of marketing, we just don't know how big that role will be.

- New technology and marketing opportunities can be challenging due to the lack of experts in these areas.

- Try new technology: It allows you to see what's out there, and you can reserve your username.

- Trying new things not only energizes your creative side, it can help engage your audience.

- Chasing trends can be a distraction to your long-term visual brand-building work.

Conclusion

"A visual always brings a first impression. But if there's going to be a first impression, I might as well use it to control the story."

—*MF Doom*

We all know visuals are important, and how we use them makes a difference. Your goal with any piece of marketing content is to get viewers to act. Luckily, there's an actual science to this, so it can be learned.

People generally respond and react in certain ways when they see certain things. Once you identify your audience and know what drives them to take action, you can create visuals to motivate them to take the action you want. This part takes time, but it will save you significant headaches in the future.

All the work you've done will help with internal buy-in

Visuals can often be swayed by personal preference. It's easy for someone higher up to say they like or dislike something. It could be a color preference or a model in a photo. Who knows what will drive a boss to give the thumbs down? But if you have the data to back up your decisions, you'll have a better chance of succeeding with selling the piece internally.

Explaining how your work compares or contrasts with competitors in your industry will show you've done your homework and identified the white space in your market. You can't stand out by fitting in. Show how you're not just mimicking what others in your space are doing and why that is a good thing.

Back in the 2010s, I ran the website for a billion-dollar company in the IT networking space. If someone suggested a change because "the industry leader does it," I made it clear that wasn't a reason to make the change. While it is a huge company, it's been a long time since that company was innovative with its marketing. We couldn't compete in that market if we tried to be just like the leader.

We needed to create content that caught the audience's attention and resonated with them. Doing persona work and measuring how the content performed allowed us to be more creative with our visual marketing. We had proven to the powers that be that we understood the audience and could craft content that would drive action.

Contrary to some opinions, it is possible to be creative within the bounds of a strong brand identity style guide. Everyone has constraints when it comes to creating content. Be it time, budget, or staffing, people always have to work within constraints. Your brand style guide is one of these constraints.

Once your brand style guide is established and agreed upon, it can speed up the creation process because you don't have to fret over which typefaces or colors you should use. Also, the style guide is a shield against executives' bad ideas. Your style guide should be revisited from time to time, but for the most part, it should be followed to establish brand consistency.

One great way to establish brand consistency and save time, effort, and money is to find new ways to repurpose the content you've already created. The hard work has already been done. Identifying ways to repurpose and reuse existing content will help you get more visual content to your audience across multiple platforms. Turn your white paper into a webinar. Or turn your blog posts into an eBook. Or turn your LinkedIn posts into a Reels video series. There are almost unlimited ways to create new content based on work you've already done. The spectrum of visual marketing assets is wider than you would think.

Creating this array of visual marketing assets requires different tools. Using the right tool for the right task may take some time to figure out. Generative AI is just another tool, like Photoshop or Canva. Luckily, there is a huge internet out there with tutorials or access to professional designers who can help you. It all comes down to whether you want to spend the time or money to create these assets.

And, of course, the future of visual marketing content creation will have some AI influence. Most software will have AI built into it, and content creation tools are no different. Your audience will let you know their tolerance level for AI-generated content. Current trends show that AI can help with some early drafts, but the result should be as organic as possible. AI can help with your audience research and localization, but it shouldn't be used to create content from scratch. Looking like everything else isn't going to get the results you want.

What's next?

If you're just creating content to check a box, AI-generated content will work. On the other hand, since you've made it this far in the book, I assume your goal is to create great content.

You know that great visual content is perfectly tailored for your well-researched audience. You measure the effectiveness of that content so you know what you should or shouldn't do next time. Sounds easy, right? It takes time, effort, and money, but the results speak for themselves. And now you understand why visual marketing is important, why it works, and how to create this high-quality content.

Visual marketing is the best way to stand out from the crowd and capture your audience's attention. There's a reason the term "eye-catching" exists. As a marketer, it's your job to capture the attention of your prospects and get them to take the next step.

If you have access to a designer or a design team, use them. They understand the foundations of creating visuals in their bones. It's hardwired into them. If your visual marketing falls to you and you have a limited budget, spend some of it on building the structure for your visual marketing. Hire a professional to solidify your brand style guide and build out your templates. Those assets, plus what you've learned in this book, will set you up for a successful future in visual marketing.

Go create some eye-catching, AND effective visual marketing content!

Acknowledgments

"Live together, die alone."

—*Jack Shepherd, LOST*

The idea for this book came to me while I was standing in Boston's South Station, waiting for my bus. I was listening to Mark Schaefer's *Known* when the idea to write about visual marketing hit me.

About nine months earlier, I started After Design to help designers adapt to an AI future. Due to the proliferation of AI, some designers would be losing their jobs, and I wanted to help them start using AI and/or find ways to transfer their design thinking skills to adjacent fields.

Then, I realized that all this design work had to go somewhere. Marketers were going to be expected to pick up the work of creating visual content. Unfortunately, they don't have the design foundation to create compelling visuals.

This book is the culmination of 25+ years of people showing me how to do things better. Without the great instructors, creative directors, bosses, and team members I've had the pleasure of working with over the years, I wouldn't be able to do what I do.

I've worked with so many great teams over the years and it would be impossible to list them all. But please know there is a good chance you've influenced my thinking on different parts of this book. Some of you may even recognize some concepts or have heard me say a few of the pithier parts of the book.

First off, thank you to Jeff Comeau for copy-editing the book. Anyone who has read my writing in the past knows that this book is much better due to Jeff's help. I used Grammarly for some proofing and ChatGPT to gut-check a couple of sentences here and there; otherwise, any AI-generated content has been noted. The rest was written, drawn, and designed by me.

Gia Manalio-Bonaventura was my accountability partner throughout this book-writing process. I first met Gia when she was my copywriting partner at my first graphic design job. Oddly enough, we worked for a book publishing company. Now, 25 years later, we're chatting about the creation of books again. She's a *New York Times* bestselling author, so I took any advice she had.

Next I want to thank the people who contributed quotes and information to the book. Hannah Szabo, Alex Tourigny, Hollie Richmond, Megan Behrendt, Chandler Quintin, Chris Penn, Laura Anthony, and many others helped expand areas that needed their unique touch. Additional thanks to Tiffani Bova and Richie Etwaru for your many years of encouragement and belief in me.

Thank you to Steve Harrington, who empowered me to build my first team of designers and creatives. I'll always be thankful for this. Vala Afshar helped me expand my career beyond design—thank you for trusting me back then and for your ongoing support and guidance.

As I mentioned, Mark Schaefer inspired me to write the book, so it was an honor when he agreed to write the foreword. The RISE community he founded has been inspirational for many areas of the ever-evolving marketing landscape.

The simple idea of writing any book wouldn't have dawned on me if it wasn't for Joe Pulizzi and his work with The Tilt, CEX, and Tilt Publishing. The team at Tilt Publishing, especially Marc Maxhimer, made this first-time author feel confident enough to upload the manuscript. Thank you to Ann Handley, whose book *Everybody Writes* taught me how to write–and how not to mix metaphors while flying this plane.

While writing this, David Armano asked how I stay so dedicated to writing. I told him it was because I had a long commute. I spend about 10-15 hours on a bus each week, and this book is how I've filled that time. Thank you to Boston Express for enabling me to be productive.

Thank you to my parents and sister for instilling the belief that I could do anything. At this point, I've figured out many of my strengths and weaknesses, but the wild idea that I could write a book came from their support when I was younger. Additional thanks to the friends and colleagues who have been there for me over the years. I appreciate you in ways you'll never comprehend.

Finally, thank you to those who inspire me the most–my wife, Jess, and my kids, Violet and Xavier. Your love and encouragement drive me to do better every day.

Jim MacLeod

Boston, Massachusetts

Notes

Introduction

4   **content with visuals is 94% more likely to be seen than text-based content:** "Visual Content Marketing Statistics: 52 Must-Know Insights for 2024," Sproutworth, January 8, 2024, https://www.sproutworth.com/visual-content-marketing-statistics/

7   **returns to shareholders are almost double those companies who don't rank well for using design:** "The business value of design," McKinsey Quarterly, October 25, 2018, https://www.mckinsey.com/capabilities/mckinsey-design/our-insights/the-business-value-of-design

Chapter 1

9   **The written language started only ~5,000 years ago.:** "Why Content Consistency Is Key To Your Marketing Strategy," Forbes, February 11, 2019, https://www.forbes.com/sites/forbesagencycouncil/2019/02/11/why-content-consistency-is-key-to-your-marketing-strategy/

23 **The firing of these synapses lead to better comprehension, retention, and recollection.:** "How Many Ads Do We Really See a Day? Spoiler: It's Not 10,000," The Drum, May 3, 2023, https://www.thedrum.com/news/2023/05/03/how-many-ads-do-we-really-see-day-spoiler-it-s-not-10000

Chapter 2

22 **Thornburg Center for Professional Development.:** "Using Images Effectively," Williams College, February 2010, https://oit.williams.edu/files/2010/02/using-images-effectively.pdf

22 **The earliest cave paintings are from 73,000 years ago.:** "These Red Crayon Markings May Be the First Known Human Drawing," Science, September 12, 2018, https://www.science.org/content/article/these-red-crayon-markings-may-be-first-known-human-drawing

23 **The written language started only ~5,000 years ago.:** "The Evolution of Writing," University of Texas at Austin, 2014, https://sites.utexas.edu/dsb/tokens/the-evolution-of-writing/

23 **The firing of these synapses lead to better comprehension, retention, and recollection.:** "Evaluation of Psychological Aspects of COVID-19 Vaccination in the General Population," Psychiatria Danubina, 2022, https://psychiatria-danubina.com/UserDocsImages/pdf/dnb_vol34_noSuppl%204/dnb_vol34_noSuppl%204_1158.pdf

23 **and increased heart rate.:** "Objective Measures of Emotion Related to Brand Attitude: A New Way to Quantify Emotion-Related Aspects Relevant to Marketing," PLOS One, November 2, 2011, https://journals.plos.org/plosone/article?id=10.1371/journal.pone.0026782

24 **Emotions = greater recall.:** "How emotion enhances the feeling of remembering," Nature Neuroscience, November 21, 2004, https://www.nature.com/articles/nn1353

32 **entice them to click and start watching.:** "Psychology Of YouTube Thumbnail Design," Video Genie, May 2, 2023, https://videogenieworks.com/blog/psychology-of-youtube-thumbnail-design/

33 **baby's brains are set up to receive information about faces.:** "Earliest look at newborns' visual cortex reveals the minds babies start with," ScienceDaily, March 2, 2020, https://www.sciencedaily.com/releases/2020/03/200302200736.htm

32 **specific part of the brain, the fusiform gryrus, that responds to faces.:** "Why Are We Drawn to Faces on Point of Sale?" Spark Emotions, November 16, 2021, https://sparkemotions.com/2021/11/16/why-are-we-drawn-to-faces-on-point-of-sale/

32 **We use faces to identify people, identify emotions, and communicate with people.:** "Beyond Face Value: How our Brain Recognizes Faces," YouTube, June 21, 2021, https://www.youtube.com/watch?v=LUsPUN6majA

32 **willing to misidentify something as a face than to miss a face.:** "Why Our Brains See Faces Everywhere," Technology Networks, July 7, 2021, https://www.technologynetworks.com/neuroscience/news/why-our-brains-see-faces-everywhere-350616

34 **they tend to be more prototypical.:** "Babies prefer to gaze upon beautiful faces," September 6, 2004, https://www.newscientist.com/article/dn6355-babies-prefer-to-gaze-upon-beautiful-faces/

35 **Juliana Stewart:** "The Scientific Reason Babies Are Entranced By Beautiful Faces," Evie Magazine, January 23, 2021, https://www.evie-magazine.com/post/why-babies-are-attracted-to-beautiful-people

36 **false information was more likely to be believed.** "Why images are so powerful—and what matters when choosing them," Bonn Institute, August 3, 2023, https://www.bonn-institute.org/en/news/psychology-in-journalism-5

Chapter 3

49 **High contrast helps us understand these elements faster.:** "The Science of Contrast," Mad Genius, February 24, 2022, https://madg.com/2022/02/24/the-science-of-contrast/

Chapter 4

62 **recalling just 10% after three days when it is just text or audio.:** "What is the Picture Superiority Effect?," simpleshow, August 9, 2023, https://simpleshow.com/blog/picture-superiority-effect/

65 **performed worse than any of their other visual content.:** "16 Visual Content Marketing Statistics to Know for 2024 [Infographic]," Venngage, December 13, 2023, https://venngage.com/blog/visual-content-marketing-statistics/

71 **anyone else can use it for their business.:** "Trademarking logos created on Canva," Canva, accessed October 2024, https://www.canva.com/help/trademarks-logo/

Chapter 5

79 **by removing distractions, people were more likely to buy.:** "10 A/B testing examples and case studies to inspire your next test," Unbounce, July 1, 2024, https://unbounce.com/a-b-testing/examples/

86 **Black people make up 15% of the US population.:** "The 15 Percent Pledge," Fifteen Percent Pledge, February 24, 2021, https://15percent-pledge.org

Chapter 6

yellow comes from a partnership DHL: X post by Ian Phillips (@ian_845846), October 25, 2023, https://x.com/ian_845846/status/1717282237203231071

Chapter 7

96 **A first-time customer can cost between 5-25 times as much as retaining an existing customer.:** "The Value of Keeping the Right Customers," Harvard Business Review, October 29, 2014, https://hbr.org/2014/10/the-value-of-keeping-the-right-customers

98 **According to HubSpot:** "27 TikTok Brands That are Winning at Marketing in 2023," HubSpot, May 22, 2023, https://blog.hubspot.com/marketing/brands-on-tiktok

106 **TikTok is on pace to surpass Facebook in total daily minutes in 2025.:** "TikTok set to surpass Facebook in daily minutes by 2025—but ad spend hasn't followed," eMarketer, September 22, 2023, https://www.emarketer.com/content/tiktok-set-surpass-facebook-daily-minutes-by-2025-but-ad-spend-hasn-t-followed

99 **TikTok's U.S. users are in the coveted 18-24 age group:** "TikTok Statistics You Need to Know," Backlinko, July 1, 2024, https://backlinko.com/tiktok-users

99 **in the U.S., 170 million people, use TikTok.:** "Love, Hate or Fear It, TikTok Has Changed America," The New York Times, April 19, 2024, https://www.nytimes.com/interactive/2024/04/18/business/media/tiktok-ban-american-culture.html

Chapter 8

108 **Coca-Cola was the 15th most valuable brand in the Kantar BrandZ 2024 ranking.:** "Kantar Brandz, 2024 Most Valuable Global Brands," Kantar Brandz, 2024, https://indd.adobe.com/view/c21c3b44-92cb-4386-848e-c1641347979b

108 **Coca-Cola's brand value is over $106 billion.:** "Coca-Cola Recovers Top 10 Global Brand Status," Marketing Week, June 14, 2023, https://www.marketingweek.com/coca-cola-recovers-top-10-global-brand-status/

110 **Coca-Cola calls its red its "second secret formula.:** "Coca-Cola Red: Our Second Secret Formula," The Coca-Cola Company, October 31, 2012, https://www.coca-colacompany.com/about-us/history/coca-cola-red-our-second-secret-formula

111   **69-90% of a consumer's initial judgment is based on color.:** "The Psychology of Colour Influences Consumers' Buying Behaviour," Ushus-Journal of Business Management, Christ University, 2017, https://journals.christuniversity.in/index.php/ushus/article/view/1761/1508

114   **great job with tying that little jingle:** ""I'm Lovin' It": The History Of McDonald's Most Popular Jingle," The Takeout, February 2, 2024, https://thetakeout.com/history-of-mcdonald-s-i-m-lovin-it-jingle-1846400888

114   **The 2024 Olympic Brand Guidelines document is 137 pages.:** "Olympic Brand Guidelines," International Olympic Committee, September 2023, https://stillmed.olympics.com/media/Documents/International-Olympic-Committee/Olympic-brand/Olympic-Brand-Guidelines.pdf

114   **General Electric's 2008 identity program was 772 pages.:** "General Electric Standards & Guidelines," Branding Style Guides, 2008, https://brandingstyleguides.com/guide/general-electric-2008/

115   **the script initials dating back to the company's founding in the 1890s – is consistent.:** "A top GE HealthCare marketing exec reveals the brand strategy that helped the GE spinoff become a $35 billion company two months after going public," Business Insider, March 13, 2023, https://www.businessinsider.com/top-ge-healthcare-marketing-exec-talks-brand-launch-2023-3

117   **without serving any other significant function:** "How Tiffany & Co. Monopolized a Shade of Blue," Artsy, April 16, 2019, https://www.artsy.net/article/artsy-editorial-tiffany-monopolized-shade-blue

117   **Tiffany & Co. has the color trademarked only in its boxes and bags.:** "The Story of the Iconic Tiffany's Blue Color," Fashion & Law Journal, October 3, 2021, https://fashionlawjournal.com/the-story-of-the-iconic-tiffanys-blue-color/

118   originally designed by the founder's wife, Marva Warnock.: "Adobe's Awesome New Wordmark Is Not Its New Logo, But Maybe It Should Be," Fast Company, June 27, 2023, https://www.fastcompany.com/90915228/adobes-awesome-new-wordmark-is-not-its-new-logo-but-maybe-it-should-be

119   Verbifying brand names comes with potential downsides.: "Google This: What It Means When a Brand Becomes a Verb," Fast Company, January 18, 2013, https://www.fastcompany.com/3004901/google-what-it-means-when-brand-becomes-verb

Chapter 9

130   pillar-based marketing saw a 22% increase in page one rankings.: "Stop Fearing Algorithm Updates. Start Reaping the Benefits," LinkedIn, August 29, 2023, https://www.linkedin.com/pulse/stop-fearing-algorithm-updates-start-reaping-benefits-ryan-brock/

138   For every podcast the team produces, they also get four YouTube videos, four blog posts, five short-form videos (at least), and nine social assets.: "AI for Podcasting with Cathy McPhillips," YouTube, November 13, 2023, https://www.youtube.com/watch?v=5EC1hahNHyk

138   ran a "no new content" challenge with its team.: "We Stopped Publishing New Blog Posts for One Month. Here's What Happened.," Buffer, August 11, 2015, https://buffer.com/resources/blog-strategies/

Chapter 11

159   In a 2022 survey: "State of Video," Vidyard, 2022, https://awesome.vidyard.com/rs/273-EQL-130/images/2022-Vidyard-State-of-Video-Report.pdf

160   Data from Emplifi: "2024 Report: Social Media Benchmarks," Emplifi, 2024, https://go.emplifi.io/rs/284-ENW-442/images/

Emplifi_Report_2024%20Social_Media_Benchmarks_EN.pdf

165   it's still growing year over year.: "Podcast Statistics You Need To Know," Backlinko, September 16, 2024, https://backlinko.com/podcast-stats#podcast-growth

Chapter 12

179   "The illusion of change.": "The Illusion of Change," Peter David, December 24, 2012, https://www.peterdavid.net/2012/12/24/the-illusion-of-change/

Chapter 13

192   Adobe acquired Macromedia in 2005).: "History of Final Cut Pro," FCP Cafe, accessed October 2024, https://fcp.cafe/learn/history/

192   Final Cut Pro was introduced as an Apple product in 1999.: "Randy Ubillos," Apple Fandom, accessed October 2024, https://apple.fandom.com/wiki/Randy_Ubillos

193   more than 40% of the collaborative design and prototyping market.: "Market Share of Figma," 6sense, accessed October 2024, https://6sense.com/tech/collaborative-design-and-prototyping/figma-market-share

193   Just a few years ago, Sketch owned 71% of the market.: "Not a Figma of Your Imagination: It's Still the Number One Design Software," Hey Reliable, September 12, 2022, https://heyreliable.com/not-a-figma-of-your-imagination-its-still-the-number-one-design-software/

194   The atomic design system.: "Creating Atomic Components in Figma," Figma Blog, November 8, 2018, https://www.figma.com/blog/creating-atomic-components-in-figma/

Chapter 14

207   **show you thumbnails that are most likely to appeal to you.**: How Netflix Uses Matching To Pick The Best Thumbnail For You, September 28, 2022, https://blogs.cornell.edu/info2040/2022/09/28/how-netflix-uses-matching-to-pick-the-best-thumbnail-for-you/

207   **Adobe also has a compensation system for contributors.**: "Firefly FAQ for Adobe Stock Contributors," Adobe, October 8, 2024, https://helpx.adobe.com/stock/contributor/help/firefly-faq-for-adobe-stock-contributors.html

209   **Chris Cox, Meta Chief Product Officer.**: "Meta is using your Instagram and Facebook photos to train its AI models," Business Insider, May 11, 2024, https://www.businessinsider.com/meta-instagram-facebook-photos-used-in-ai-models-training-2024-5

211   **This led to a 10:1 return on investment (ROI).**: "Case Study: Creative Programmatic Display for Publishers," Admixer, January 28, 2016, https://blog.admixer.com/creative-programmatic-display/

211   **Asmita Dubey, L'Oréal chief digital and marketing officer:** "How L'Oreal is tapping generative AI to transform its marketing," SiliconANGLE, April 11, 2024, https://siliconangle.com/2024/04/11/loreal-tapping-generative-ai-transform-marketing/

212   **an important part of the human condition.**: "Content Marketing Questions Answered (Special Episode)," YouTube, October 4, 2024, https://www.youtube.com/watch?v=hE4UzhvGd70

Chapter 15

214   **short but engaging videos appeal to a growing audience.**: "Stats and Trends Defining Visual Marketing in 2024," SlideShare, March 12, 2024, https://www.slideshare.net/slideshow/stats-and-trends-defining-visual-marketing-in-2024/266745825?from_search=0

215   **keep the core elements of their visual identities intact even when they adopt trendy visuals.**: "Mountain Dew's new logo returns to its Appalachian roots," Fast Company, October 9, 2024, https://www.fastcompany.com/91203861/mountain-dew-logo-branding

218   **The video is displayed in 16k resolution and has to be cut into slices to fill the space.**: "How Do You Think the Graphics Are Made for the The Sphere in Las Vegas?" Reddit, November 16, 2023, https://www.reddit.com/r/AfterEffects/comments/17wj086/how_do_you_think_the_graphics_are_made_for_the/

Index

Author Bio

Jim MacLeod is a seasoned digital marketing leader with over two decades of experience helping businesses craft compelling brand experiences. With a bachelor's degree in Graphic Design and a master's degree in Marketing, Jim has built a reputation for seamlessly blending creative strategy with data-driven insights to drive measurable results. It has been said that his superpower is the ability to identify the most important part of any marketing material and ensure the viewer sees it. His expertise spans brand strategy, digital marketing, and visual design, making him a sought-after voice at the intersection of marketing and technology.

Jim has held leadership roles at tech companies across all stages—start-ups, growth, and established industry leaders—and has experience on both the agency side and within B2B and B2C companies across various industries. This breadth of experience gives him a unique perspective on driving growth through creative strategy and digital transformation. Known for fostering highly collaborative teams, Jim cultivates environments where creativity and innovation thrive, resulting in improved outcomes and more effective campaigns. He is passionate about understanding customer needs and crafting strategies that drive action, leading to stronger, more authentic brand experiences.

A lifelong New Englander, Jim loves going on adventures with his wife and two kids.

Reviews and Praise

"The Visual Marketer is a brilliant visual design and strategy playbook written by one of the most creative and talented digital marketing leaders in the world. Jim's wisdom is practical, actionable, and valuable for all marketers."

—Vala Afshar, Chief Evangelist at Salesforce
and former CMO of Extreme
and Enterasys Networks

"When I started in magazine publishing, I learned that the most important thing about a magazine is the cover. The cover's job is the most important... to get people to turn the page. The same is true for nearly all content today. If your content is not visually appealing, good luck getting people's attention. The good news for you? Jim covers the what, why, and how of visual marketing in this book. You don't realize how much you need the content inside this book."

—Joe Pulizzi, Bestselling author of *Content
Inc.* and *Epic Content Marketing*

"As marketing becomes more crucial to business success, design remains a core element. Jim distills his decades of experience at the forefront of design into an easy-to-follow, practical guide. Whether you're a beginner or an expert, this roadmap will help elevate your design skills and take your marketing to the next level."

—Richie Etwaru, CEO, Mobeus

"Jim MacLeod has a unique ability to simplify design for marketers. In *The Visual Marketer*, he breaks down the essentials of visual strategy, making it accessible for anyone looking to improve their marketing results through better visuals. This book is a must-read for marketers who want to build their design confidence and drive impact."

—Tiffani Bova, Executive Advisor, WSJ
Bestselling Author of *Growth IQ*
and *The Experience Mindset*

"The infinite scroll has wholly transformed how our attention is grabbed and retained, and the future of marketing is visual. Jim MacLeod takes us through the basics and advanced aspects of visual media, which has become the dominant form of marketing through advertising, brand building, or influencer partnerships. *The Visual Marketer* is like a physical, hand-held ChatGPT, which will help you crack the visual marketing code."

—David Armano, Senior Marketing
Executive and Visual Strategist